Contents

Maintrack Meanderings
    The Overlander –   Auckland to Wellington   2
Moonlight Express
    The Northerner –   Auckland to Wellington   10
The Evening Special
    The Kaimai Express –   Auckland to Tauranga   12
Best Kept Secret
    The Geyserland –   Auckland to Rotorua   15
Seeking out the "Sun-Seeker"
    The Bay Express –   Wellington to Napier   18
Bridging the Gap
    The Inter-islander –   Wellington to Picton   22
Between Mountain and Sea
    The Coastal Pacific –   Picton to Christchurch   24
Mountain Pass
    The TranzAlpine –   Christchurch to Greymouth   29
Deep South Sojourn
    The Southerner –   Christchurch to Invercargill   35

Route Map – inside back cover

**Grantham House
New Zealand**

Maintrack Meanderings
The Overlander – Auckland to Wellington

Auckland. City of sails. Protector of the Americas Cup. The largest Polynesian city in the world. New Zealand's largest city by far. If you have just arrived in Auckland, there are a thousand and one activities in which to indulge before beginning your train trip on The Overlander, one of several long-distance trains operated by Tranz Rail Ltd under the Tranz Scenic brand. You can sail the Hauraki Gulf, sip Espresso amidst the burgeoning café society of the central city, shop, visit museums and unique one-offs like Kelly Tarlton's Underwater Sea World.

Auckland has its own casino, so a little spending money can be won on the side. A ferry trip from downtown Auckland to the "suburban" island of Waiheke is a highlight – a celebration and affirmation of a sea-dominated city. Rail enthusiasts seeking an entrée before The Overlander main course would be well advised to travel on the Auckland to Waitakere suburban service run by Tranz Metro, a line that travels right across the city to the foothills of the Waitakere Ranges in the west.

Kevin Ward

The Overlander itself departs from Auckland station at 8.30am every day, immediately confirming Auckland's marine aspect as the line crosses the wide expanse of Hobson Bay by causeway, before rolling through suburban South Auckland.

It has been said that to begin your train travels through New Zealand on The Overlander from Auckland, is an ideal, modulated way to immerse yourself in the character of the New Zealand landscape. Scenic highlights are, of course, an individualised phenomenon; beauty is in the eye of the beholder. However, it seems appropriate that the traditional "biggies" such as the central volcanic plateau of the North Island, the maritime aspect of the Coastal Pacific route and the alpine "excesses" of the TranzAlpine should not be encountered at the outset. They would be hard acts to follow, scenically, if you encountered them all early on, at the very beginning of a rail odyssey with Tranz Scenic.

Mind you, the initial stretches covered by The Overlander are worth the price of admission alone. Talk of the North Island "main trunk" is invariably reverential. The main trunk, linking New Zealand's largest city with the capital, Wellington, is very much the bottom line in terms of New Zealand railway heritage. It is a route not to be trifled with.

The Overlander, within the first hour of its journey, takes a while to extricate itself from the urban sprawl. Despite New Zealand's image of being dominated by wide open spaces and lonely green rural holdings, over 80 per cent of the population live in cities, and about one third of such city dwellers live in Auckland. This city, in terms of area and extension, is one of the largest in the world, a legacy of the New Zealander tradition of home ownership. Many of these homes have taken root on generous, individually owned sections of land. It has been said that New Zealanders have no head for heights: skyscrapers are relatively thin on the ground, and massed apartment dwelling is still comparatively rare.

Auckland has also been described as the Los Angeles of Australasia, not because of any established movie or celebrity industry, but because of its car fetish. This has, over the years, translated into an inability to come to terms with the need for a coordinated rapid-rail commuter service. From the train window one can observe cars heading towards the city snarl on the motorways and suburban approach roads. Passengers on The

Just north of Ohakune, the south-bound Overlander crossing the modern concrete Hapuawhenua viaduct.
D.L.A. Turner

Overlander can afford to feel smug as the train accelerates beyond such traffic congestion.

Eventually, the suburbs recede and the line encounters the rural greenness that visitors have come to expect. At Paerata, just north of Pukekohe, the industrial branch line serving the Pacific Steel mills at Mission Bush arcs away. This is also Glenbrook Railway territory, an interesting diversion for rail enthusiasts. The Glenbrook Vintage Railway is one of the longest established of New Zealand's restored railways, with its own distinctive rolling stock and an ongoing steam engine restoration programme. The most recent triumph, particularly for steam buffs, is the reincarnation of Ja 1250, a sleek, powerful engine that, along with the K class, used to dominate the everyday rail landscape of post-war New Zealand.

The green gives way to brown, as the market gardens surrounding the town of Pukekohe are broached. It is only a temporary aberration before the vast expanse of farmland associated with the northern Waikato. The Waikato River, New Zealand's longest, soon enters the picture too, with the main trunk meeting this mighty, slow-moving body of water at the township of Mercer.

Mercer station these days is a comparatively modest affair. Passenger services, including The Overlander, no longer stop here. And yet Mercer station, at its zenith in the post-war years, was a hive of activity. It is fair to say that even back then, the station enjoyed a status out of all proportion to the size and significance of the town. Many years earlier the large, shambolic station had been the railhead on the line from Auckland. The proximity of the wide, navigable Waikato River made it possible for south-bound travellers to catch a paddle-steamer, after alighting from the train, and float down the Waikato as far south as Cambridge. Beyond Mercer the line passes through the Whangamarino wetlands, a protected conservation area. At this point the double-tracked main trunk splits for several miles, testimony to the difficulties experienced

The south-bound Overlander passing through fertile farming country near Owhango in the King Country.
D.L.A. Turner

when a solid road-bed was sought for the line.

The Waikato River reappears at Rangariri, and soon we reach the coal-mining centre of Huntly. The spectacular rail bridge over the river here still carries coal trains, but they are a far cry from the steam-hauled demons of earlier eras. These days the coal trains are sophisticated diesel-drawn monsters which carry the coal from the mines west of Huntly, back up the main trunk where they are switched to the branch line serving the Pacific Steel mills.

The first major stop on the line is the city of Hamilton, an attractive, progressive centre dominated by the Waikato River. It is New Zealand's largest inland centre. After living with a "cow-town" tag for several decades, Hamilton is now acknowledged as a sophisticated, cosmopolitan city with many attractive features.

Hamilton has a growing reputation as the home of some of the most innovative gardens in New Zealand, and tours linking such attractions are freely available. It is said that Hamilton is built on grass. The warm weather, regular rainfall and peat soils provide a perfect combination for grass growing. Friesian and jersey cows turn the grass into milk, as a result of which a world-beating dairy industry has emerged.

As a reflection of this international status, every June thousands of farmers and visitors from all over the world attend the New Zealand National Agricultural Fieldays at Mystery Creek, just south of the city. Special trains have, in recent years, carried interested parties from Auckland to Hamilton to attend the event.

A few kilometres further to the south-east is the town of Cambridge, base for some of the most successful horse studs in the world. Cambridge Stud, until recently home of the legendary stallion Sir Tristram, sits on 500 acres of flat, rich grassland and has been developed into a thoroughbred showpiece.

Perhaps the most arresting feature of Hamilton is, however, the Waikato River which flows slowly through the city's heart. Apart from Wanganui, no New Zealand city can boast such a dramatic river environment. The Tranz Scenic "Waikato River Cruise and Gardens" day trip from Auckland makes the most of this feature by including a cruise on the Waipa Delta, a restored paddle-steamer.

Rail enthusiasts will also find Hamilton something of a Mecca. By basing themselves in the city for a day or two, they can catch The Kaimai Express to Tauranga and back, as well as ride on The Geyserland to Rotorua, another day trip. In this sense Hamilton is a genuine passenger junction, the only centre where more than one Tranz Scenic service radiates away from the main line.

South of Hamilton The Overlander travels over territory that used to be treacherous swamp and peat bog. During the construction of the track it took hundreds of construction workers three years to link Frankton with Te Awamutu. One of the major problems was a massive, seemingly bottomless hole in the swamp near the settlement of Ohaupo. More than a hundred tons of debris were swallowed up, causing considerable delays.

At the same time New Zealand was beset with a national fear of Russian invasion. This rather unlikely link with the railways impacted on construction progress by drawing away many of the work gangs to shore up coastal settlements against the perceived Russian threat. In the case of the work gangs on the main trunk south of Hamilton, this meant redeployment to Devonport to help install gun battlements.

After the Rukuhia Swamp, dairy-farming country creates a rich green tapestry. The land of milk and money, as someone put it, is upon us. Te Awamutu is a well-appointed, thriving centre with a growing reputation as the rose capital of New Zealand, to go with its dairying status. Indeed, Te Awamutu is often referred to as Rosetown, and its rose gardens and farm-stay amenities provide incentive to break your journey for a day or two.

There didn't use to be much reason for trains to stop at Otorohanga, in the days between the "bad" old days of express train travel and the resurrection of the upgraded Tranz Scenic services. These days, of course, it is the gateway to the famed Waitomo Caves and other attractions in the hinterland beyond the main trunk line. Adventurers doing Tranz Scenic's Train Day Escape from Auckland, called "Caves and Kiwis", leave The Overlander at Otorohanga to boat through the silent waters of the Waitomo Caves lit by glow-worms, before visiting the Kiwi House and Native Bird Park and returning by train to Auckland in the evening.

If making their own way down the North Island, perhaps using a Best of New Zealand pass to travel around by train and coach, day two of an itinerary could see visitors rejoin The Overlander at Otorohanga to journey as far south as National Park. Bush walks, skiing and adventure activities await them here, along with the spectacular scenery provided by the central volcanic plateau and Mounts Ngaruhoe, Tongariro and Ruapehu. Furthermore, they get to extend the sheer pleasure of travelling by train through some of the most riveting scenic grandeur in the North Island.

There's a lot to be said for travelling in this manner. Not only do you see the world class attractions that would otherwise remain hidden and inaccessible beyond the hills and mountains, but the staggered nature of such travel means you set out each day to catch the train refreshed and relaxed. Such "discoverers" are able to rejoin The Overlander

The north-bound Overlander passing through Oio with the majestic snow-clad Mount Ruapehu on the horizon.
Kevin Ward

An aerial view of the famous Raurimu Spiral looking across the Waimarino Plateau towards National Park from near Raurimu, with the mountains Tongariro, Ngauruhoe and Ruapehu on the skyline. Tranz Rail

on day three of their itinerary and travel, bright-eyed and bushy tailed, on the third hop to Wellington.

Towards midday The Overlander passes through Te Kuiti, the archetypical King Country railway town. Te Kuiti is now better known as the shearing capital of the world: no one shears sheep faster than the scions of the local farming community. The annual Te Kuiti muster, held in April, is fast becoming a significant event on the New Zealand tourist calender. The extravaganza, now incorporating the New Zealand Shearing Championships, features the best shearers in the world and is an appropriate advertisement for a distinctively New Zealand activity.

Te Kuiti is an attractively appointed township set in the valley of the Mangaokewa which began as a railway construction camp in 1887. The town is an alternative stopping off point for visitors to the Waitomo Caves, as well as providing several farm-stay options on the large holdings that spread over the rugged landscape.

Taumarunui station, next stop down the track, is still a substantial edifice. Its significance to the lifeblood of the main trunk was profound, and when in 1975 the old refreshment rooms were closed, the occasion was marked by the attendance of a large proportion of passengers off the Auckland to Wellington Express. Together with one hundred local Taumarunui residents, the passengers crammed into the refreshment rooms to mark the closing of an institution in New Zealand railways history. Here in a field still stand a selection of decaying steam locomotives waiting hopefully for restoration.

Some thirty minutes further south is another institution of New Zealand railways: the Raurimu Spiral. Thousands of words have been written about the Raurimu Spiral: how the line needed to rise over 200 metres to meet its obligations and join Raurimu with National Park, in such a way that a train could

Heartland hinterland: The Overlander tiptoes past a slumbering Mt Ruapehu. Tranz Rail

reasonably negotiate such an incline.

Raurimu is one of the most awe-inspiring spiral complexes in the world. Thirty-four kilometres beyond Taumarunui The Overlander reaches the edge of the volcanic plateau. Back in 1898, when the line was being built, this physical conundrum offered up several alternatives. One was to skirt the problem and add 20 kilometres of track and nine additional viaducts to carry the main trunk up to the rarefied heights of the central plateau. Then along came an engineer named Robert Holmes who devised a devilish alternative. Basing his plan on overseas encounters with such physical obstacles, he proposed constructing a spiral which would wind and climb along the edges of the escarpment at a respectable gradient of 1 in 52. Although such an alternative would require sharply curved bends, five embankments, two tunnels and one complete circle, it seemed to make more economical and logistical sense than 20 kilometres of extra track and a swag of viaducts.

It was a gargantuan engineering feat, involving as it did more than three complete turns as the line climbed dramatically above the township of Raurimu. And it didn't come cheaply. However, its novelty value for train enthusiasts and travellers in general has doubtless led to its paying its own way several times over since it was opened in 1907.

In 1997, as The Overlander attacks the spiral, an air of excitement pervades the carriage. The passengers have certainly heard of the Raurimu Spiral. Indeed, one claims that the "eighth railway wonder of the world" is one of the principal reasons for his being on the train. And the other seven? I guess we'll never know. Certainly not while The Overlander screams around the tight spiral curves in what someone else claims are "ever diminishing circles".

The climbing, the rate of ascent, is tangible. In a sense time and forward motion stand still as the spiral takes the train up to the wide, mountain-studded plateau. The thrill of the spiral is soon replaced by the overwhelming

From a great height: The Overlander crossing the Makatote viaduct. Tranz Rail

sight of the three snow-clad peaks: Ngaruhoe, Tongariro and Ruapehu.

The fact that all three mountains have been active volcanoes adds to the awe-inspiring scene. Tongariro has been quiet for a while but Ngaruhoe erupted in the 1960s, and Ruapehu has been active in the 1990s. The notion that volcanic activity could begin on Ruapehu at any time proves alluring for many travellers. I recall an earlier journey down this route just a year before, when Ruapehu, quite against predictions, puffed out a high column of volcanic smoke and ash, on cue seemingly, as the train hove into view. The entire Overlander population was utterly transfixed on that occasion, although it was impossible not to recall the fury unleashed when Lake Taupo was formed, admittedly thousands of years ago. On that occasion the volcano that stood where Lake Taupo now laps innocently, disappeared in an explosion five times bigger than Krakatoa in 1883.

Many passengers alight at National Park or Ohakune. Visitors can tramp through this incredible landscape, sample the rarefied air or ski the slopes of Ruapehu. For some the notion of skiing down the slopes of an active volcano is just about the ultimate challenge.

Further south Makatote, the last and highest of the original viaducts built during the course of completing the main trunk, carries the train virtually into mid-air. At 258 feet it is the second highest viaduct in New Zealand. Along with the Makatote, the Makohine, Toi Toi, Hapuawhenua, Waiteti and Manganui-o-te-Ao, viaducts provide another spellbinding series of attractions on this most ambitious railway line. Despite this grandeur and significance, the monument erected to celebrate the driving of the last spike – the completion of the mighty North Island main trunk – is something of an understatement.

Further down the track Ohakune, once a rail settlement in the middle of nowhere, has been transformed into a ski resort town with many upgraded buildings, modern chalets and restaurants to cater for the visitor market.

Of all the towns on The Overlander route, Ohakune has undergone the most profound transformation. The Turoa ski field is just up the road, and thousands of visitors flock to the area each year.

The train is now travelling due east past the Karioi State Forest towards Waiouru, the highest station on the line and the setting for one of New Zealand's largest and certainly most isolated army camps. The QEII Army Memorial Museum is another Waiouru landmark.

As we swing towards the south the line descends. The central plateau begins to give way to rolling hill country. We reach Taihape just after 3.30pm, and it too has undergone something of a transformation – though not as dramatic as Ohakune's – and is developing into a holiday town for those who hanker for a get-away-from-it-all experience amidst the peace and tranquillity of a truly rural environment. Tranz Scenic run a "Gone Bush" segment in their "Great Train Escapes" package, and for city slickers and overseas visitors wishing to experience the wide open spaces and good home-cooked country food, it appeals as a unique alternative. "Gumboots under glass" won't feature on the menu, but the annual gumboot-throwing contest provides a tongue-in-cheek reference to Taihape's farming origins.

South of Taihape the line travels through the distinctive Rangitikei region. Mangaweka, perched on an escarpment above the Rangitikei River, marks the upper reaches of a physical landscape that is best remembered for its unusual eroded, grey papa rock cliffs.

At Marton Junction the line changes course again, this time heading south-east towards the Manawatu Plains. Marton is still a genuine rail junction, with the line to Wanganui and New Plymouth continuing up the west coast.

Before long we are passing through some of the most fertile areas of the world, supporting burgeoning sheep and dairy farms and related pastoral industries. Finally, our cross-country jaunt ends as The Overlander pulls into Palmerston North. From here on it is basically due south for the final sector of the journey. Depending on the time of year, the sun may have already set. Or you may be lucky to witness a spectacular sunset as the train travels through the Horowhenua region and down the Kapiti Coast, past ever-increasing urban conglomerations to the north of the capital city, Wellington.

Irrespective of the season you choose to travel, the final stanzas of the journey are memorable. As The Overlander emerges from the tunnels of the Tawa Deviation you are either assailed by the late-afternoon, picture-postcard beauty of Wellington Harbour or the glittering lights of the city by night. Either way, it is a fitting conclusion to a remarkable odyssey, one that has taken you across the roof of the North Island on one of the world's great rail journeys. Auckland now seems light years away.

The Overlander south of Utiku heading south to Wellington. D.L.A. Turner

Moonlight Express
The Northerner – Auckland to Wellington

If you are a fan of night trains, and many travellers are, The Northerner running between Auckland and Wellington (and vice versa) is a must. Not only is it New Zealand's sole overnight train (it has been described as the "soul train"), but it has an atmosphere uniquely its own. And of course, on a practical level, it is an ideal way to save on the price of overnight accommodation or make up time in a busy itinerary.

The Northerner in summer provides a kaleidoscopic view of suburban sunsets, but somehow the service seems more valid taken in the depth of the New Zealand winter. You leave in darkness and arrive in darkness. That, according to many travellers, is part of the appeal of night trains.

The days (or nights) of sleeping cars have vanished from the New Zealand rail scene, but the cosy reclining seats will lull all but the most hardened insomniac. The soporific swish and sway of The Northerner's momentum will assist in sending you off to dreamland.

Many people indulge in night-train travel just to savour the atmosphere: the sacred darkness of the heartland of New Zealand; the flickering lights of small-town, backblock dwellings; the amiable company of fellow travellers, many of whom gravitate to the café counter for a nocturnal snack and inevitable cup of coffee.

Fellow traveller Ben McCormack, a veteran of night-train travel on the Auckland to Wellington Express, is taking The Northerner rather than The Overlander daylight service, simply for sentimental reasons, although he would never describe his motivation in such terms.

"The overnight express was part of my heritage. I practically grew up on those night trains. They represented freedom to me and my mates. The sly boozing, the sing-a-longs, the stampede to the refreshment rooms. We used to play games with the crockery. Used to bowl the cups along the platform. See how far they would go before disappearing under the carriage wheels. A bit dangerous, I guess.

Those cups were so solid they could have caused a derailment. Then there was "flying saucers", with saucers being hurled like the discus into the darkness. You could hear them coming. They made a funny whistling sound. Mind you, because they were white you could see them coming too, which meant that no-one got seriously hurt."

Just before midnight The Northerner stops at Te Kuiti, deep in the heartland. The station

lights flicker as several hardy souls, bundled up against the weather, board the train. Lights pulse around the local pie-cart where nocturnal stock agents and shearers gather for something sustaining.

Doug Hutchins, my father, came to Te Kuiti just before the Second World War. He still lives there with his vivid memories of what the arrival of night trains meant to a town like Te Kuiti.

"Back in the '30s, when a steam train seemed to have a personality, the local station became the town's social rendezvous. In midwinter when the 7.15pm Auckland to Wellington Express arrived, the station was invariably packed. Years passed and steam gave way to the impersonal diesels. The latter exuded a rank diesel odour that permeated clothing and left you branded for some hours as a diesel addict."

Doug, now 84, tells another story about the pure magnetism of the railways, in days when it was the biggest show in town: "I remember a small laddie, not yet four, who disappeared early one morning. He was missing from his bed at dawn and immediate panic set in. After a fruitless search the phone rang. Dire news was expected. The call came from the local taxi driver ringing to say that a very small lad was sitting on the railway station watching the 5.40am Wellington to Auckland Limited preparing to leave. Luckily the local taxi driver knew me and my family well. It was my son who had gone trainspotting at three years of age and 5am. The lure of the railways, particularly the night trains was a powerful force."

Somewhere up on the central plateau, a vividly clear moonlit night throws the high ground into shadowy relief. You imagine you can see the mountains off to the left. The café counter continues to serve snacks and coffee. Passengers, some yawning, others looking remarkably fresh, still traipse through, for companionship as much as anything.

A grey dawn breaks somewhere beyond the Tararuas, for the passengers who are still awake to see it. The Northerner skirts the Kapiti Coast as the day gradually turns fine and clear.

Back up the track the small towns, provincial cities and rural outposts of the heartland have already started their day, largely unaware that several hundred perfect strangers tiptoed through their backyard on The Northerner in the middle of the night. Night trains can be stealthy track-mates.

Late in the afternoon, The Overlander crosses the Paremata bridge on the last leg of the journey to Wellington. Tranz Rail

The Evening Special
The Kaimai Express – Auckland to Tauranga

The Kaimai Express departs Auckland at 6.05pm, so, in winter anyway, it is essentially an evening train journey of little more than three hours' duration. Its late scheduling allows for a stopover in Tauranga, with the return trip undertaken the following morning. The return Kaimai Express departs Tauranga at 8.05am, arriving back in Auckland at 11.40am.

You can't travel on The Kaimai Express without becoming aware of the impact of the Kaimai Tunnel on the train's journey and very existence. And yet the tunnel's genesis did not lie in any consideration of passenger traffic facilitation.

It became obvious that the existing line between Tauranga and Paeroa would be incapable of handling goods traffic projected to be in excess of one million tonnes by the mid-1970s. To this end the decision was made to construct the Kaimai Tunnel, a bold scheme that would see the distance between Rotorua and Tauranga shortened by 62 miles, and that between Hamilton and Tauranga by 32 miles. At the same time, feasibility studies relating to the overall development of the Bay of Plenty, an industrial and forestry growth area, suggested that a new line be built from Rotorua to join up with the Bay of Plenty line east of Tauranga. Although this would increase the distance between Hamilton and Rotorua, travelling time would decrease. This particular development, yet to be acted on, is a question of need times resources equalling political opportunism.

The need for the Kaimai Tunnel, however, had been established. Now it was simply a matter of digging a hole through the base of the mountain – that and a new stretch of track. The path to the tunnel, the length of line running from Waharoa on the Rotorua branch, through the tunnel as far as Apata on the Bay of Plenty line, is still the newest stretch of railway in the Tranz Rail system. Train buffs with an obsession to cover as much "virgin" track as possible are acutely aware of the fact when they travel on The Kaimai Express.

The 8.9-kilometre tunnel, the longest in the southern hemisphere, and deviation line between Waharoa and Apata began operations on 12 September 1978. The tunnel was constructed by the Ministry of Works and Development for the New Zealand government and was opened by the prime minister of the time, Robert Muldoon. Nearly twenty years later the tunnel has become as Kiwi as corrugated iron, as much

The Kaimai Express heading east towards Tauranga. Tranz Rail

The Kaimai Express on the Tauranga Harbour Bridge.
Tranz Rail

a part of the rail landscape as the Raurimu Spiral and the Midland line.

My companion on The Kaimai Express was an elderly gentleman named Burt who looked somewhat out of place. He would have been more at home surrounded by the old NZ Rail crockery, pie wrappings and slabs of fruit cake, his white hair tousled and flecked black by coal smoke from the old Ab steam engine hauling the train. In those days it could have been the mixed goods train to Tauranga graunching across the same tracks.

"I used to go to school by train, along this very track," reminisced Burt as The Kaimai Express gathered speed beyond Morrinsville. "In the old days I was what they called a train boy. I cycled three miles from the farm to catch the morning train which deposited us at Hamilton Station at 9am or thereabouts. Shunting duties along the line often dictated arrival times. I caught the train at Rukuhia. Then it was another half mile walk to school from the station. Caught the train home again at 3.30pm. Always arrived home in the dark in winter, with a bike ride through the night to complete the journey."

We were now speeding through the Kaimai Tunnel, and the sudden darkness added emphasis to Burt's observations.

"Every time the train stopped, boys would jump off and find a patch of grass to play 'test' cricket or rugby on. We felt like the All Blacks on tour. Playing in a variety of venues. The thing was back then the engine would do a bit of shunting at just about every stop. It made for a long journey and a lot of footie. The engine driver always gave us a warning toot when it was time to go. Often it was quite unfair. You'd be hot on attack and the bloody train whistle would go. We reckoned the driver'd been bribed with gob-stoppers by the other side on more than one occasion. Mind you, there was no negotiation. Often there wasn't even time to retrieve a lost football or cricket ball and you'd have to mount a search on the way back, on the return train. All Black trials were often staged along the tracks. I was always Maurice Brownlie. Always. Never got dropped."

We had by now exploded from the Kaimai Tunnel and after veering south, the outskirts of Tauranga were upon us.

Tauranga is one of the most exciting train

destinations in New Zealand. Not only is it a burgeoning commercial and industrial city, drawing on the primary products of forestry and farming from further inland, but it remains one of New Zealand's most popular seaside resorts. In fact, together with neighbouring Mount Maunganui, it can be described as one of the most sought after holiday destinations for thousands of New Zealanders and an expanding number of overseas visitors.

Tauranga's railway environment is like no other in New Zealand in terms of convenience. The Strand railway station sets passengers down a few metres from the harbour's edge, where ferries and other craft are readily accessible. It is also right in the heart of the city. A brief walk from the train and you will have touched base with hotel, motel or guest house.

The Tauranga Harbour rail bridge adds to the dynamics of this sea-fringed rail setting. At this stage The Kaimai Express doesn't travel beyond the Strand station (and that means missing out on a trip across the harbour bridge), but perhaps one day such a highlight could be scheduled into the train's route.

The Geyserland Express crossing the Waikato River at Hamilton en route to Auckland.
Kevin Ward

Best Kept Secret
The Geyserland – Auckland to Rotorua

It has been said of trains in general that they often ply areas of country inaccessible by road, or at the very least cover alternative routes to those taken by familiar highways. This is never more apparent than when travelling on The Geyserland from Auckland to Rotorua, between destinations that have been travelled on numerous occasions – by road.

The Geyserland and its antecedents have a proud history. On 5 May 1930 the Rotorua Limited made its first journey between Auckland and Rotorua. It soon developed a reputation, comparable to that of The TranzAlpine of today's fleet, as a world class "name" train. Rotorua's fame as a tourist Mecca in the antipodes fuelled the popularity of the Rotorua Limited. Back then, in pre-adventure tourism days, the thermal wonders of Rotorua and its hinterland were regarded as essential viewing by the travellers of the day. And until the end of World War II, trains were the most appropriate and convenient means of shifting large groups of geyser-seeking visitors.

In this climate the popularity of the Rotorua Limited (or Rotorua Express as it later became) burgeoned. In the early days of its operation it even boasted a wide-windowed observation car, but with the incursion of Railways Road Services buses, the Express lost ground.

The Rotorua Express was fitted out as an excursion train, with Oriental carpet in the observation car, silver fittings, ornate blue silk curtains and rich upholstery. Individualised electric lights, electric fans and ceiling ventilators, and wind-proof concertina vestibules between the carriages enhanced passenger comfort. It was a far cry from the spartan condition of most New Zealand trains of the time. The present-day railcar provides a comfortable journey with sheepskin seat covers, air conditioning and food served at one's seat, among other amenities.

The Geyserland could fairly be described as Tranz Scenic's best-kept secret – certainly along the section from Hamilton to Rotorua, which affords many unexpected highlights. Of course for those travelling on the line from Auckland to Hamilton for the first time, there are all the scenic features of the northern sector of the North Island main trunk to savour. Auckland, the maritime city, the Whangamarino wetlands, the mighty Waikato River and the Huntly Power Station are just a few.

At Hamilton The Geyserland moves on to the Bay of Plenty line or simply "the line to the east". Following a momentary plunge beneath the commercial heart of Hamilton, the train roars out over the Waikato River with its ancient, deep waters flowing far below. The eastern suburbs of Hamilton recede, and the straight run to Morrinsville commences across the highly fertile Waikato Plains.

Morrinsville used to be a thriving junction with trains carrying on through to Te Aroha and Thames on the Thames branch. The Taneatua Express, a railway institution in the post-war years, also touched base at Morrinsville before branching off at Paeroa to travel the long way round through the Bay of Plenty. The advent of the Kaimai Tunnel has put paid to any similar future meanderings, although services had been abandoned long before the tunnel's construction. And then there was the Rotorua Express, or its later Fiat railcar equivalents,

Kevin Ward

15

which veered off to the railhead of the Rotorua branch.

Prosperous dairy farms and factories dominate the physical and industrial landscapes as the train swings across country to the junction settlement of Waharoa. Here the Tauranga branch can be seen angling towards its rendezvous with the Kaimai Tunnel.

A little further down the track is the rural servicing town of Matamata, a leafy, well-established settlement. It wasn't always like this. Josiah Clifton Firth, one of the original founders of the town, leased vast tracts of land from the Maori and by 1884 held 56,000 acres. On much of this he carried out intensive drainage of the swamplands that had thwarted local development. He was also responsible for building a road to the military settlement at Cambridge and made the Waihou River navigable, enabling Te Aroha to be developed as a port. A remarkable man, he even found time to write the first published New Zealand play, a political satire called "Weighed in the Balance" (1882).

Appropriately, given the thermal nature of The Geyserland's destination point, Matamata provides something in the way of an appetiser. The Opal Hot Springs near the town provide private hot mineral pools as well as substantial public baths, and the Crystal Hot Springs feature an air-conditioned indoor fresh-water pool, heated by thermal water, set in picturesque picnic areas.

Just beyond the small town of Tirau the thermal theme continues. At Okoroire, the Okoroire Hot Springs Hotel, an old-world charmer, provides a tranquil setting, hot mineral pools and a 9-hole golf course for some time-out with a difference.

We reach Putaruru Junction at around 11.30am. Here The Geyserland swings to the east towards the Mamaku Ranges, while the short branch to the south of Putaruru serves the paper mill at Kinleith and forest products in general from the Tokoroa area. Putaruru grew up as a timber town, and its major industries feed off the vast

The Geyserland with Lake Rotorua in the background.
Tranz Rail

exotic forests in the hinterland.

From Putaruru to Rotorua The Geyserland follows a course not shared by the highway. As a result some very different forestry settings and rural backwaters catch the eye. At times it is hard to believe that a few miles to the north State Highway 5 covers basically the same distance, over remarkably different terrain.

For visitors and locals who think they've been to Rotorua, a trip on The Geyserland will convince them that perhaps they haven't. The climax of the rail journey is an easy winner over the road option as well. As The Geyserland finally emerges from the forested hills beyond Mamaku, Lake Rotorua suddenly appears in all its reflected glory down in the Rotorua Basin.

Like all famous rail journeys, half the fun occurs when you reach your destination. Rotorua has always been a tourist Mecca. Indeed, it has been said of Rotorua that this is where this country's tourism began. According to this theory, the tourist industry in New Zealand grew out of international curiosity about the geothermal wonders of the central North Island. People from the civilised world travelled around the globe by sailing ship and horse-drawn coach to see the Pink and White Terraces of Tarawera. Even the destruction of the terraces in 1886 did not deter visitors, who couldn't get enough of the spectacular geysers, hot bubbling mud and steaming pools of boiling water. In addition there were therapeutic reasons for travelling which highlighted the spa aspect of Rotorua. To add to the allure of the city, Rotorua was also regarded as the heartland of Maori culture, and the village of Te Wairoa, buried during the 1886 eruption, is now a tourist attraction in its own right as "The Buried Village".

One of the most famous of the early Rotorua hotels was "Brent's" which appropriately is now the site of the Hyatt Kingsgate, one of the leading hotels and convention centres. In 1880, with government backing, a spa was built at the Maori village of Ohinemutu to tap the priceless thermal resources. In 1907 a European-style spa complex was created for the treatment of physical ailments. That building, named Tudor Towers, now functions as the district museum and art gallery.

In the 1990s Rotorua's thermal wonders continue to fascinate: the massive geysers and bubbling mud, unique rock and land formations and steam drifts. In recent years adventure tourism has become a growth industry. There are gondola and luge rides; four-wheel drive expeditions to witness the broken beauty of Mt Tarawera, the volcano that erupted spectacularly towards the end of the last century; helicopter and plane rides over this and other notable landmarks; boat trips including lunch on the Lakeland Queen paddle-steamer on the substantial Lake Rotorua that dominates the Rotorua basin; day trips to the other lakes surrounding Rotorua; and outings to Fairy Springs with its teeming trout population and wildlife parks.

And of course, as in the halcyon days of the Rotorua Express, when the taking of the thermal waters was regarded as just about the trendiest pastime you could dabble in, the soothing waters of the Polynesian Spa in modern day Rotorua are not to be missed.

The enduring memory of a trip on The Geyserland is the way that a comparatively unsung train journey can provide so many scenic surprises and unexpected twists and turns. It is perhaps Tranz Scenic's best-kept secret.

Prestige trains meet – The Geyserland and Kaimai Express passing at Ngaruawahia. Kevin Ward

Seeking out the "Sun-Seeker"
The Bay Express – Wellington to Napier

The Bay Express is another New Zealand treasure, a six-hour trip between the capital, Wellington, and the provincial centre of Napier in Hawke's Bay. Even fellow New Zealanders are astounded at the distinctiveness of the landscape, with the views beyond the train windows often taking on the hue and outline of some impressionist painter. The preliminaries to these scenic masterpieces have their own charm.

Of course, Wellington isn't merely the beginning of the line to Hawke's Bay, certainly not for train enthusiasts. While the capital city abounds in attractions like cafés, city tours, historic pubs, art galleries, the recently opened Museum of New Zealand (Te Papa), sophisticated shopping and Parliament Buildings, it also boasts the most complex and interesting suburban rail network in New Zealand. A day or two spent travelling the Wellington commuter lines is a must for true train fans.

For a start the historic Johnsonville line (it used to serve as the initial stretches of the old main trunk out of Wellington) climbs up through the bush-clad hills of suburban Ngaio, Khandallah and Johnsonville. The most picturesque suburban line in New Zealand, it immediately takes on a character of its own as it winds back into the hills overlooking the capital. Then there is the Hutt Valley line which skirts the harbour before following the course of the Hutt River towards the foothills of the Rimutaka Mountains.

Intrepid train travellers who catch the service to Masterton in the Wairarapa will carry on beyond the Hutt Valley, through the mighty Rimutaka Tunnel (it is only a couple of chains shorter than the Kaimai Tunnel, making it New Zealand's

The Bay Express stretching out along the Kapiti Coast. Tranz Rail

second longest), before curling up through the Wairarapa Plains. The historic townships of Featherston and Carterton rattle past before the train terminates its journey at the provincial centre of Masterton.

If you really want to dot your "I's" in terms of touching base with all Wellington suburban lines, don't forget the truncated spur to suburban Melling. Commuter services also run north to Paraparaumu and Palmerston North over the main trunk that carries The Overlander, Northerner and Bay Express.

The Bay Express departs Wellington every day at 8am. Beyond Wellington station the train follows the harbour rim for a time before veering inland through the two long tunnels of the Tawa Deviation. The darkness of the tunnel provides a chance to collect thoughts, after something of a scramble to get to the departure point on time, to familiarise yourself with carriage fixtures and make a nodding acquaintance with fellow passengers.

Back in the daylight The Bay Express, which features forward-facing and table-seating carriages, a café counter and a rear window viewing area, follows the main line north through the suburbs of Wellington. The Tasman Sea and the harbours and estuaries remain in the picture for much of this section of the journey. For us it is a fine, clear morning and the sun climbing over the headlands reflects off the incoming tide.

Once out of the Tawa tunnels, which effectively take the train underneath the suburb of Newlands, The Bay Express makes its first stop at Porirua. The line then hugs the eastern shoreline of Porirua Harbour and crosses the causeway at Paremata, before cutting inland.

Pukerua Bay comes into view as the line meets the rugged Tasman coastline. For the next few kilometres the train slinks along the cliff face affording magnificent ocean views and, on clear days, glimpses of the South Island. Kapiti Island, a bird sanctuary, sits moored off the coast.

We pass commuter trains taking workers into the city and feel slightly smug that we have been temporarily freed from the workday shackles to indulge in the pleasures of Tranz Scenic. Beach resorts that also double as dormitory towns flash past as we gather speed: Plimmerton, Paekakariki, Paraparaumu, Waikanae. Paekakariki is of special interest to rail fans.

Steam Incorporated runs a museum featuring the reincarnation of a main line locomotive depot and workshop at Paekakariki. Steam and diesel locomotives

The Bay Express threads its way through the Manawatu Gorge.
Tranz Rail

and a vintage train are also available for excursions and charters. A programme of restoring the old Paekakariki station building has also attracted a lot of interest from rail fans. A tramway museum is another local attraction.

The Bay Express gathers speed as we pass through the Horowhenua towns of Otaki, Manakau and Levin, home of some of the country's most bountiful market gardens and orchards. The fertile Manawatu Plains are now beneath our wheels, and the myriad dairy farms provide evidence of the basis for the region's prosperous dairying industry.

Just after 10am the train pulls into Palmerston North, a major junction city of 80,000 people and home to Massey University, world famous for turning farming into a science. Palmerston also boasts the Grasslands Division of the Department of Scientific and Industrial research, the Palmerston North Seed Testing Station, the NZ Dairy Research Institute and the Awahuri Artificial Breeding Centre. Agricultural science is a cornerstone of the city and environs economy and activity.

Palmerston North's rail history is distinctive too. The first railway linked the settlement with the port of Foxton, leading to the development of the economy and social base of the inland town. Despite this, Foxton remained the leading community in the area. Originally the plan was to build a line from Wellington to Foxton, but eventually in 1880 the services of the largest private railway company in New Zealand were summoned. The Wellington-Manawatu Railway Company decided to forge the link between Wellington and Palmerston North for parochial and political reasons. The logical extension of the main trunk north, through Foxton and Bulls, was axed in favour of the course along the foothills of the Tararuas. As a result of this twist of fate, and bend in the line, Palmerston North and not Foxton became the dominant population centre of the region.

Palmerston North these days is a sophisticated, cosmopolitan centre with a well-established New Zealand and overseas student population. Many fine restaurants and farm-stay holidays are available, as well as amenities like museums, art galleries and parks. A museum with a difference is the Rugby Museum, a growing shrine to New Zealand's national sport. The scope of exhibits is truly international, and the museum is the recognised leader in its field.

Beyond Palmerston North, as The Bay Express at last begins its journey on to the Hawke's Bay line, we come to the Manawatu Gorge. The gorge, a geological oddity, is often cited as the main reason some passengers travel on The Bay Express. It is geologically remarkable in as much as it was formed by the corrosive action of the Manawatu River which rises in the eastern Ruahine Ranges before cutting back through the North Island's backbone to reach the sea on the "wrong" western coast. That backbone is currently moving upwards, while erosion is slicing down through the rocks, producing the decidedly steep-sided gorges, to which road and rail cling. The railway line through the gorge is an engineering feat of herculean proportions.

Woodville, just beyond the gorge, is the consummate junction town. Here both road and rail from the Wairarapa link with routes from the Manawatu and Hawke's Bay. Woodville was originally called "The Junction" and later evolved into Woodville, a reference to its location in the once dense Seventy Mile Bush.

The latter, a giant totara forest, also dominated the original Scandinavian settlement at Dannevirke where The Bay Express is scheduled to arrive at 11.17am. The service centre for a prosperous mixed-farming region, Dannevirke is notable for its sedate pace and gracious old homesteads. Not surprisingly, sawmilling was its growth industry in the very early days and this, along with the arrival of the railway in 1884, led to the rapid development of the town and its hinterland.

The line The Bay Express plies came comparatively early to the Hawke's Bay. Construction commenced from Napier in 1872, and the initial miles over open plain presented few problems. By 1878 the line had reached Kopua, 62 miles from Napier. From here, however, the obstacle presented by the Seventy Mile Bush, together with broken country and deep gullies, slowed progress. During this phase the Ormondville viaduct was constructed, and the town of Ormondville itself took shape.

One of the highlights for rail enthusiasts on this stretch of track is the Ormondville railway station restoration project, an ambitious scheme that has faithfully recreated a typical country railway station of the 1950s and operates as a bed and breakfast establishment.

The hills begin to flatten out beyond Takapau as the Takapau Plains dominate the landscape. Waipukurau, centre of one of the most flourishing sheep farming regions in New Zealand, continues the Central Hawke's Bay residential characteristic of stately old homesteads and an appearance of established rural graciousness.

The Takapau Plains give way to the Heretaunga Plains, a highly fertile region that lays claim to being the most bountiful pip-fruit country in the world. The concentration of three large rivers, the Tukituki, Tutaekuri and Ngaruroro, has led to the deposit of alluvial silt, the raw material for such fertile expanses. Vineyards and market gardens also take advantage of nature's windfall and, based on such bounty, wine making and sophisticated cannery operations contribute to a flourishing export industry.

Watties frozen food and canning factory is one of the most prominent features of the city of Hastings, which The Bay Express reaches at 1.05pm. Hastings is one of two back-to-back Hawke's Bay cities (the other, Napier, is another twenty minutes down the line), and many passengers begin their exploration of the hinterland here.

Finally the "art-deco" capital of Napier is upon us, a laid-back centre of vineyards and wine tasting, art-deco tours and antique shops, beaches and marine attractions. The architecture of Napier is like that of no other New Zealand city. As a result of the devastating earthquake of 1931, the city was rebuilt in the architectural style of the day known as art-deco and, rather like the restored villa splendour of Dunedin, which transports you back in time to the beginning of the century, the distinctive stylings of Napier trap you in a time capsule of their own.

In little more than five hours The Bay Express has transported us from the capital, with much of it clinging to the surrounding hills, through the backbone of New Zealand, to a city that has as much character as any on earth. That, together with the long and winding wine trails, make for a heady train journey.

Over Ormondville: The Bay Express crossing the Ormondville Viaduct. Tranz Rail

Bridging the Gap
The Inter-islander – Wellington to Picton

Long-distance submarine rail tunnels can be uninteresting, sterile environments, a claustrophobic interlude in what may have been a perfectly enjoyable daytime train journey. There has often been talk of linking the North and South Islands, particularly in terms of rail continuity, as New Zealanders reminded themselves that a stretch of water called Cook Strait would not go away as an ongoing obstacle to travel.

Luckily for travellers on the Tranz Scenic circuit, there is still a need to travel by ferry between the two islands. That ferry journey on The Interislander service is often cited as being one of the true highlights of any rail pilgrimage through New Zealand.

Ironically, The Interislander isn't a train, nor is it a boat train, but an integral part of the Tranz Rail transport network. It offers one of the world's outstanding scenic cruises as it plies the waters of Cook Strait. All three vessels of The Interislander link are roll-on, roll-off rail ferries, providing foot passengers and passengers with cars, motorbikes, campervans and other vehicles with a safe and enjoyable break from train travel.

The *Aratere*, *Arahura*, and *Arahunga* of the Interislander fleet are no tubs. They are fully equipped ocean-going vessels that cover the 96.36-kilometre journey in little more than three hours. The service operates every day of the year, and it is a rare occurrence when sailings have to be cancelled because of adverse weather.

After travelling by train from Auckland to Wellington, the Cook Strait crossing affords a wonderful opportunity for reflection and relaxation. The Interislander ferries provide a range of first-class amenities that compliment such "time-out" from train travel. Each ship provides a restaurant and café, movie theatre, entertainment area, information office and travel shop, lounge, bar, children's area and nursery.

Perhaps the highlight of the ferry crossing is the peaceful waters of the Marlborough Sounds, similar in many respects to the Norwegian fjords. The ferry enters the Sounds through Tory Channel before negotiating the deep Queen Charlotte Sound.

For those travellers who want to cross the strait with more alacrity the *Lynx* service, a 74-metre catamaran that operates in summer, is capable of linking Wellington with Picton in one hour, 45 minutes. The *Lynx* is one of the fastest passenger and car-carrying links in the world and features at-seat service, climate-controlled cabin temperatures and complimentary TV entertainment.

The Arahura *in quiet waters of the Marlborough Sounds.*
Tranz Rail

Time out between Islands. The Arahura *sailing up Queen Charlotte Sounds.* Tranz Rail

Between Mountain and Sea
The Coastal Pacific – Picton to Christchurch

Maritime train journeys are highly sought after diversions. The Coastal Pacific, running from Picton in the north to Christchurch, the largest city in the South Island, is about as maritime as a train journey gets. The shore-hugging stretches of The Coastal Pacific's route are an obvious highlight of the five-hour journey, but the line offers a variety of landscapes and some unusual twists as well.

Like all Tranz Scenic trains The Coastal Pacific has a flavour of its own. There is no other service that features such maritime scenery. There are times when you feel as though you are travelling on a fast ferry, such is the proximity of the train to the boiling Pacific Ocean. The pounding breakers become mesmerising as the salt spray flays the carriage windows and the sheer magnitude of the seascape fills your senses.

There are other times, of course, when the ocean settles like a millpond, on clear diamond-bright days. The steady swells become soporific. Whether stormy or idyllically calm, the ocean aspects of The Coastal Pacific's route are overwhelming.

The opening stanzas of the trip are fascinating enough but give little warning of what is to follow. Picton is a quaint town nestled deep in the Marlborough Sounds – Queen Charlotte Sound to be precise. Much of its significance derives from the fact that it is the inter-island ferry terminal, providing a mooring berth for the vessels that link Wellington in the North Island with Picton in the south.

Picton is also the first landfall for an area of New Zealand that has become known as the gourmet's paradise. Mussels, olives, salmon and world-class wines are abundant. Wine-trailing and café-hopping are strenuous local exertions. The Nelson-Marlborough region is also famous for its high density of artists and craftspeople and has more galleries and craft shops than just about any other region of New Zealand. The more adventurous can tackle the Queen Charlotte Walkway, dabble in sea-kayaking and fishing, set out on four-wheel-drive

Not much to come and go on: road and rail share a pittance of coastline. Tranz Rail

The Coastal Pacific hugging the coast. Tranz Rail

safaris and mountain-bike scrambles in the interests of working up an appetite or working off the excesses of the gourmet trail.

As The Coastal Pacific commences its journey from Picton, immediate levitation is needed to cross a saddle that shields the town from the southerly winds. As the train scores a path into the hillside, each turn offers tantalising views across the settlement to the sparkling waters beyond.

The path offered by a rail journey is non-negotiable. Thus, there is time to reflect on the world outside as it pans across the viewing windows. Here man's puny influence on the landscape looks back at you, and little has changed over the decades apart from the cutting of road and rail.

Beyond Elevation, The Coastal Pacific descends on to the Wairau Plains where the townships of Koromiko, Tuamarina and Spring Creek flash past. Crossing the Wairau River, the train passes into wine country. Blenheim, principal town of the Marlborough region, is the first stop. Essentially a service centre, Blenheim has also become in recent years the capital of the Marlborough wine-growing industry. The high sunshine hours and suitable soils have turned the region into a wine-growing centre of developing international stature, particularly in relation to Sauvignon Blanc. The option of a stopover in Blenheim is a must for wine lovers. It is also the gateway to the "Top of the South", with access to Nelson and the West Coast.

Parched hills dominate the landscape as the train pulls out of Blenheim, heading due east for a distance. Eventually the line curves south-east through the Dashwood Pass, across the Awatere road-rail bridge, before stopping at the small town of Seddon. The road-rail bridge is quite remarkable and the only one of its kind in New Zealand. It is two-storeyed with trains running on the upper level and cars on the lower.

Lake Grassmere, the centre of New Zealand's salt-making industry, springs out of nowhere as the line descends to sea level. Massive lagoons trap sea water where the high sunshine hours enable evaporation to produce thousands of tonnes of salt every year for domestic supply. The train is dwarfed by the white salt mountains as the line bisects the massive operation. Beyond the salt works, Marfell Beach and the Cape Campbell lighthouse merge with the horizon.

Ward and Mirza rush past and the train crosses the Waima River before suddenly emerging on the coast at Wharanui. The impact of the wide expanse of the Pacific is breathtaking. For nigh on 100 kilometres The Coastal Pacific will hug the coast, in a manner unique to New Zealand train travel and with very few equals anywhere.

As the Pacific Ocean enters the frame to the left, the Inland and Seaward Kaikoura Ranges dominate the skyline to the right. Beyond the mountains Molesworth Station and Langridge, Upcot and Camden Homesteads occupy some of the loneliest backblocks in New Zealand. The Coastal Pacific route has the main Blenheim to Christchurch highway for company at this stage, and seals will soon be visible beyond the rocks. The hamlets of Kekerengu and Parikawa pass before we reach Clarence on the Clarence River. By now the Seaward Kaikoura Ranges tower above us, virtually forcing the train into the ocean. Waipapa Bay, Mangamaunu and Hapuku are tiny isolated settlements sitting in the lee of the mountains to one side and the cusp of the coastline on the other. At times there isn't room to swing a cat or "toss a tinny" as the friendly Australian sharing our carriage reckons.

North of Kaikoura, crayfish vendors have set up stalls and caravans to peddle the popular armour-plated delicacy to passing motorists. The outskirts of Kaikoura are upon us, and after a breathtaking ride, we stop for a five-minute rest at the "Crayfish Capital".

Many travellers alight at Kaikoura to have a closer look at the seals, dolphins, whales and other marine life. Some will be flying over the whales' domain as a guest of Whale Watch

The Coastal Pacific heading north between mountains and the sea. Tranz Rail

Air. Others will take a boat tour with international award winners, Whale Watch.

Kaikoura has always held a certain fascination. Long before the sperm whale, seal and dolphin operations came into being on the back of emerging adventure tourism, Kaikoura stood out as being rather special. A town with character. Perhaps it was the fact that it was pretty much halfway between Picton and Christchurch and the only town of consequence along this isolated stretch. It was certainly famous, even then, as the crayfish capital of New Zealand. And then, of course, it had not one but two mountain ranges watching over it in the form of the Inland and the Seaward Kaikouras.

As The Coastal Pacific heads south from Kaikoura, with the Kaikoura Peninsula receding in the distance, there is an expectation that the railway will soon be cutting inland to link up with the darkening recesses of North Canterbury. And yet the hugging of the Pacific Coast continues, down past Goose Bay to Oaro. Here the main road weaves inland at last, yet the railway clings defiantly to the coast. We are in remote territory now as the dying glow of the sun and vast shadows cover the endless whitecaps.

Finally, at the Conway River, the line at last angles away from the sea towards Hunderlee. The parting is sudden and final and you begin to wonder if you dreamed all that has gone before: the expansive ocean vistas, the snow-capped Kaikoura Ranges, the incredible engineering feat that pushed the line through in the first place. It is surprising to learn that the Picton to Christchurch link was not completed until the end of the Second World War. It is more difficult to understand why it hasn't become a national institution, the entrenched path for some annual pilgrimage. Or merely an excuse to head south.

On a more practical, concrete note, The Coastal Pacific route features the largest number of concrete bridges along any section of railway in New Zealand. This represents no

Crossing the Awatere road-rail bridge. Tranz Rail

The Coastal Pacific in clearing weather. Tranz Rail

forward thinking on anyone's part, just a bit of a steel shortage when the line was being constructed. The highest of such concrete structures is the Okarahia Viaduct, between Claverley and Oaro, officially known as Bridge Number 96.

When we crossed the Conway River, we passed, in provincial terms, from Marlborough into Canterbury. Hawkswood, Parnassus, Mina, Domett, Motunau and Omihi rush past as the light begins to fade across the North Canterbury Plains.

The next settlement down the line is Waipara, a significant junction centre, with the road over the Lewis Pass branching off here. This used to be the rail junction for the old NZ Rail branch line to Waiau, not far from Hanmer Springs. Luckily for rail enthusiasts and visitors alike, the Weka Pass Railway has recreated much of the ambience of this archetypical New Zealand branch line of the 1950s. It is a genuine excursion railway, complete with red oxide painted wagons, restored carriages, a traditional bright red guards van and an old (88 years of age) steam locomotive, A 428. A 428 has had a brilliant career, at one time (in the 1900s) hauling the prestigious Rotorua Express.

Beyond Amberley the familiar build-up of dormitory towns and service centres heralds the approach of Christchurch. Rangiora, just beyond the Ashley River, Kaiapoi, home of the woollen mills, and then the northern suburbs of Christchurch are upon you – Papanui, Bryndwr, Fendalton – affording glimpses of homes and gardens as The Coastal Pacific passes through suburban backyards on its approach to the city. Finally the train arrives at Christchurch and, despite the grandeur of the day, the knowledge remains that for those staying around the city for a day or two, much remains to be experienced.

Pack your bow tie (for the casino) and your binoculars (for the Port Hills gondola) and enjoy these as well as Christchurch's other attractions, including riding the trams, visiting the Antarctic Centre, wizard watching (binoculars optional), or simply shopping and enjoying a night on the town.

For others it will be a matter of resting up between trains and contemplating the magnificence of The Coastal Pacific route. It's that sort of train journey.

Mountain Pass
The TranzAlpine – Christchurch to Greymouth

Much has been written about The TranzAlpine, the Tranz Scenic service running through the Southern Alps to the West Coast and back. This "Great New Zealand Rail Adventure", rated as one of the top six scenic train journeys in the world, has not lacked for superlatives. You would be forgiven for thinking that a certain amount of overkill might be inherent in much of the praise. If the trip is so marvellous, how is it that NZ Rail didn't cash in on the godsend in earlier decades? The Midland line from Christchurch to Greymouth, and train services using the route, weren't exactly household names back then. But these days, around Christchurch, the name TranzAlpine is dropped as readily as icons like Mt Cook and Queenstown.

The journey on The TranzAlpine all the way from Christchurch to Greymouth fully lives up to its reputation. The beginnings are innocent enough. Departure from the modernistic Addington station at 9am is uneventful, although the size of the train surprises – usually at least seven carriages, invariably fully booked.

The southern suburbs of Christchurch provide a timely reminder that the city remains the central focus of a well-established agricultural economy. To this end, fertiliser factories, wool stores and manufacturers of

The TranzAlpine at Springfield station. Tranz Rail

Above: *The TranzAlpine in its element.* Tranz Rail

Oppostie page: *Snow shrouds the Upper Waimakariri.* Tranz Rail

agricultural equipment dominate the industrial landscape. People industries are in the mix too: Templeton Hospital and Rolleston Prison. Rolleston is also significant for being the junction, the hallowed point at which the magnificent Midland line hives off at 80 degrees to the main line south, bound for glory.

For many New Zealanders on our journey this is the first time they've travelled on this line. Train travel in the South Island in the past usually meant a bumpy, sleep-deprived hike from Christchurch to Dunedin on the old overnight express. Now, in the glistening mid-morning, they are heading towards the mountains with great expectations.

The plains don't break up immediately, but there is a perception that we are rising. Our English antecedents have left their mark on these rural reaches with names like Aylesbury, Kirwee and Sheffield. At 10am, one hour out from Christchurch, The TranzAlpine pulls into Springfield. Despite the fact that the train appeared full at departure time, it is now being asked to accommodate a swag of backpackers who appear to have come down from the hills.

Springfield represents the edge of the plains and the end of the conventional Canterbury landscape, as we have known it so far. With very little fanfare and even less effort the diesel engine hauls The TranzAlpine into the mountains, by negotiating the awesome Waimakariri Gorge and edging its way around the Torlesse Range. In a very short space of time The TranzAlpine climbs to a head-spinning height as the scenery turns wondrous.

The majesty of the line's construction and engineering become obvious. Sixteen tunnels and five viaducts ease the passage of the train through the gorge. The wilderness is magnificent. The open-air observation car on The TranzAlpine provides a vantage point for photographers as all the sights and sounds of a genuine mountain railway hit the senses. At this stage the railway is doing what it often does best: following a course into landscapes of physical grandeur that roads cannot follow – or match. Up here in the wild reaches of the Waimakariri only the train, to wit The TranzAlpine, goes.

Beyond the gorge the line eases to the west through evocative-sounding places like Avoca, Craigieburn and Cass. Cass, in fact, represents a return to the real world in a sense,

for here we meet up again with the main highway from Christchurch to Greymouth and the upper reaches of the Waimakariri River.

The braided course of the Waimakariri is now so wide that the occasional settlement, chalet and lodge on its far-off banks seem like miniature toys. Everything is dwarfed by the immensity of the landscape. As The TranzAlpine snakes around bends, the bridges and viaducts we have already negotiated look like match-stick models as the massive main divide closes in and glowers down.

Geologically we are reminded that the upthrust nature of all this rugged grandeur didn't just occur because "Our Maker" decided it would be character-building, that it would present a bit of a challenge to have a bunch of mountains running down the middle of the South Island. In more earthy terms the Southern Alps are the result of a grinding collision between two of the earth's biggest tectonic plates. These plates, and the mountains on which they sit, are moving at the rate of 2.5 centimetres a year. How that will impact on Tranz Scenic timetabling remains to be seen – it will probably come down to which way the mountains are moving!

Beyond Bealey, where we leave the Waimakariri for the last time, the steepling gorges and bare, barren rock open out, revealing stands of tussock and a greening effect on the mountains that seems to be operating in reverse of the alpine progression we were taught in school. As The TranzAlpine climbs towards Arthur's Pass, it is as though we are tiptoeing across the very roof of the South Island.

Finally, we enter an enchanted zone: Arthur's Pass township and station, set in a narrow cleft in the towering snow-clad mountains – 737 metres above sea level, no less. A truly alpine railway setting, this could be Switzerland or Austria. The Southern Alps rise on all sides; holiday baches, at one time tunnel-workers homes, share the valley floor with permanent residences. Arthur's Pass station resembles a chalet and has back-to-back platforms. Passengers of all nationalities spill out to soak up the unique rail environment, for a short break before the train forges

The TranzAlpine crossing Kowai Bridge near Springfield.
Tranz Rail

westward. A number of passengers, many of them travelling on day excursions from Christchurch, leave the train at Arthur's Pass. The day excursionists will be making the most of their five-hour allotment before the returning TranzAlpine picks them up in the late afternoon. For such passengers their day excursion includes the viewing of displays and audio visuals at Arthur's Pass before undertaking alpine walks in Arthur's Pass National Park. Depending on fitness levels and weather conditions, Devil's Punchbowl or Bridal Veil, and a four-hour marathon through the Bealey Valley await to test sinew and lung capacity.

There is no doubt that the train has reached the halfway mark in its journey across the backbone of the South Island. As Arthur's Pass is left behind, the line plummets on a 1-in-33 gradient to the next stop at Otira. It is a dramatic drop, much of it played out in the confines of the 8.5-kilometre Otira Tunnel. When it was opened on 4 August 1923, it was the longest rail tunnel in the British Empire. Today, thanks to the completion of the Kaimai and Rimutaka Tunnels, the Otira is now only the third longest, but not by much.

The highway, in typical fashion, goes over the top of Arthur's Pass while the rail, in the grip of the Otira Tunnel, goes under it. Once we are out of the tunnel, the West Coast assails us. The Otira Tunnel has been like amnesia. Suddenly we are in a new micro-climate, a new time zone almost – certainly a different world. Rain forest sprouts on all sides of the track, except where settlers have had the intrepidity to clear fell for grazing cattle and build houses where thick bush used to stand. Closer to areas of population like Greymouth, town supply dairying units have taken root.

The contrast between what we are now winding through and that which has been left behind on the other side of the alps is total. Coming down to earth, the vegetation born of a massive rainfall is essentially West Coast. In keeping with high rainfall totals, lakes abound, many of which are reported to teem with trout.

Speaking of water, as we pass through Inchbonnie it is interesting to learn that this isolated hamlet has a rainfall figure of over six metres per year. It's certainly not measured in inches. Perhaps Metrebonnie would be a more appropriate, if less appealing name.

Beyond Inchbonnie Lake Brunner appears

The Tranz Alpine heading for Greymouth between Aickens and Jacksons on the West Coast. D.L.A. Turner

out of the podocarp forest. Moana railway station, set on the shores of the lake, qualifies as one of the most picturesque New Zealand stations. The peace is tranquillising. The TranzAlpine stops here but you get the distinct impression that it doesn't want to leave.

After leaving the enchanting shores of Lake Brunner, the line threads its way through Kotuku and Kokiri towards its rendezvous with the Grey River. This is absolutely West Coast now. Stillwater, near the Grey, is true to its name: areas of water, not quite lakes, abound. The Grey River, however, is by no means still. Stillwater is a junction town too, with the line through the Buller George branching off here. In the good old days of refreshment-room stampedes Stillwater was very much "time for refreshments" – last chance for a pie and cuppa before hitting Greymouth twenty miles down the line.

The West Coast owes its commercial existence to coal and gold, and latterly to forestry and tourism. But there's more to it than that.

For those who have never been to the West Coast of the South Island, the experience will almost inevitably be one of fascination and surprise. The territory beyond Greymouth has a rough-edged charm and an obvious history, born of coal-mining days, gold dredging and an often unforgiving climate. For many it is like stepping back in time to the way things were for most New Zealanders in post-Second World War years. That's not to say the area is trapped in a time warp, more an open-handed tribute to the fact that a lot of the human values retained on the coast hark back to more homely, warmly reminiscent times for many New Zealanders caught in the fast lane. Nostalgia can be said to be a growth industry on the coast, simply because settlements like Greymouth, Westport and Hokitika continue to look like the "good" old New Zealand.

Sadly for rail enthusiasts, the once-burgeoning arteries of West Coast railways no longer exist. Coal trains still make it across the Cobden Bridge over the Grey River, and a comparatively recent development has seen

With the backdrop of the Alexander Range in the Southern Alps, the TranzAlpine, Christchurch-bound, is seen leaving Stillwater. D.L.A. Turner

the introduction of massive coal trains feeding off the Ngakawau coal fields, before carrying the black gold on to the Midland line all the way to Lyttleton Harbour, east of Christchurch, for export. But there is still evidence of the various branch lines and inclines, and a day or two can be devoted to checking out the old Rewanui incline to the north of Greymouth and the township of Blackball, which used to boast its own branch line from Ngahere, across the Grey River.

Near Greymouth the restored village at Shantytown provides another slice of West Coast history. A faithfully restored gold mining town set at the turn of the century, it features an authentic bush railway propelled by "Kaitangata", an Fa class locomotive.

Despite its timeless charm, with tours to the ancient Punakaiki rocks and gold-panning adventures, the West Coast also caters for "adrenalin" generations with jet-boating, bush-walking, caving, cave tubing and white-water rafting. Greenstone is also a unique feature of the West Coast raison d'être.

People with vested interests in the precious stone don't exactly pray for earthquakes, but a reasonable shake often means the production of significant amounts of the "hard-as-steel" stone. It's all about what happens when an irresistible force meets an immovable object with rock being sandwiched between your average tectonic plates. That's when jade, or greenstone, or pounamu, gets real. Earthquakes are nature's way of mixing up a batch of greenstone. "Every quake has a greenstone lining" as some local had it.

Much of the spectacular scenery through which The TranzAlpine travels also owes its existence to the grinding of tectonic plates. The TranzAlpine route, an ocean-to-ocean jaunt across the great divide, presents so much scenic diversity that many tourists claim the return trip, Greymouth to Christchurch, is necessary to take it all in. And even then it can still be too much to absorb.

Recognition of the 231-kilometre journey was not long in coming. In 1988, its first year of operation, The TranzAlpine won a New Zealand Tourism Award in the Tourist Section, and as recently as 1997 Tranz Scenic won the New Zealand Tourism Award in the Transportation Section and the Supreme Award. The part played by The TranzAlpine in these awards was not insignificant.

Deep South Sojourn
The Southerner – Christchurch to Invercargill

The Southerner, running from Christchurch to Invercargill, is one of the more established of the Tranz Scenic long-distance services, having been introduced as a going concern by the former NZ Rail in 1970. It is also one of the most substantial. Apart from The Overlander and The Northerner plying the North island main trunk, no train covers such a vast distance. It stops at eleven towns and cities during the course of its nine-hour journey and functions not only as a visitor attraction but also as a vital communication link across the long miles (by New Zealand standards) between Christchurch and Invercargill, New Zealand's southernmost city.

The Southerner also functions as a gateway to Stewart Island, New Zealand's "third" island, and the lonely ramparts of South Westland. Tranz Scenic has developed a "Great Train Escape" package, incorporating passage on The Southerner, to enable travellers to soak up the atmosphere of New Zealand's wild but beautiful "forgotten coast" south-east of Balclutha.

And not surprisingly, The Southerner, is the obvious rail link to the launching pad for Stewart Island. Following a night in Invercargill, a twenty-minute flight the next morning gets you to Stewart Island, which remains one of the few New Zealand destinations that many locals haven't visited.

The great appeal of travelling on The Southerner lies in the knowledge that the stretch covered by the train is the oldest in New Zealand's rail history. By 1879 the link between Christchurch and Invercargill was complete, at a time when the North Island main trunk from Auckland had only reached as far south as Te Awamutu.

Mind you, that's not to say the southern link was a coordinated push south with a single-minded objective of reaching "Bluff or bust". The line had its genesis in provincial railways, leading to the completion of isolated sections that eventually fused into a trunk railway.

At the outset it took two days to cover the link from Christchurch to Invercargill. Today's Southerner manages the same trip in nine hours, gaining a head start by dint of the flatness of the Canterbury Plains where mixed cropping and sheep grazing dominate the rural landscape. There are magnificent views of the snow-capped Southern Alps as we head across the plains. The line barely bends until the approaches to the Rakaia River bridge. The Rakaia River bridge is by far the longest rail bridge in the country, measuring 5720 feet in length. Following heavy rain inland the river can swell dramatically to fill the wide expanse of what is normally an empty, braided river bed.

The relentless charge south continues across the Canterbury Plains, the closest analogy New Zealand has to the mid-west of the USA. High speeds are maintained, and you begin to wonder if The Southerner will ever stop, or even slow down. Eventually, over an hour out from Christchurch, the train pulls into Ashburton, a substantial rural-serving town in the heart of Mid Canterbury.

In towns like Ashburton you feel the aura of the "old" New Zealand. This is not frontier territory like the rugged reaches encountered a similar distance south of Auckland on the North Island main trunk. Down here passing motorists still wave at the train, and many of the buildings have a timeless quality.

For rail enthusiasts this is also branch-line country. Nowhere else in New Zealand did tendrils from a main trunk branch so rapidly as they did along the Christchurch to Invercargill line. Little rail activity remains today, although regular excursions run along the Pleasant Point railway, a preserved stretch of the Washdyke to Fairlie branch, and, further south where the Taieri Gorge Railway has re-enacted much of the Central Otago line's character. But there are still mute reminders of the halcyon branch-line days of Canterbury, Otago and Southland. For the serious rail enthusiast, a day or two exploring the old embankments and relics (in conjunction with the guidance provided by David Leitch and Brian Scott in their book *Exploring New*

The Southerner above Karitane travelling south-bound through Puketeraki. D.L.A. Turner

Zealand's Ghost Railways) will provide an interesting diversion.

An example can be found at Tinwald, just south of Ashburton, where the old branch line to Mt Somers and Springburn used to head inland at right angles. Further exploration can be made of the Hornby to Southbridge and Little River, Rakaia to Methven, Studholme to Waimate/Waihao Downs, Pukeuri Junction to Kurow, Waiareka Junction to Ngapara, Palmerston to Dunback, Milton to Roxburgh, Mosgiel to Outram and Balclutha to Tahakopa branches, together with the complex series of rail arteries that once fed the heart of the Southland region.

The Southerner continues speeding south, through Winslow, Windermere and Hinds before roaring across the Rangitata River on a bridge that, while it isn't a patch on the Rakaia, is still ranked as the fourth longest in New Zealand. While the train has been on its straight-as-a-die rush across the plains, it has been possible to take advantage of the central tables that separate the two sets of passengers sitting opposite each another. The terrain is ideal for writing postcards and letters, without the diversion of sharp cornering, and enjoying morning tea and brunch-like snacks without the threat of spillage.

"Special meals can be ordered at the time of reservation (diabetic/wheat-free/ vegetarian) for purchase on board." This Tranz Scenic catering edict, as it appears in brochures and timetables for all services, is bearing fruit for the two women sitting opposite us enjoying a vegetarian dish as the line finally begins a long arc to the east, towards the sea.

At 10.20am we reach the city of Timaru where we encounter the blue Pacific Ocean for the first time. Caroline Bay beach resort has the look of a well-established summer holiday retreat, the Atlantic City of the South Island. You can imagine Caroline Bay at the turn of the century, or earlier, after the rail link between Christchurch and Invercargill had been established, with young men and women sporting long, coy, woollen bathing suits, playfully gambolling in the shallows. There is a distinct sense of history along this stretch, certainly as old as New Zealand's European heritage gets.

Timaru is also a stopping-off point for travellers bound inland for Lakes Tekapo, Pukaki and Ohau, and, further on, Lakes Hawea, Wanaka and Whakatipu. And, of course, Mt Cook, New Zealand's highest, is accessible on the highway from Timaru to Lake Pukaki.

A walk in the Oamaru Public Gardens is also recommended, while in the evening a stroll to nearby Cape Wanbrow will be richly rewarded. This is where the little blue penguins come ashore, and the sight is a fascinating one.

As The Southerner climbs away from Oamaru the plains are left behind, and the climb around the rugged Otago coastline will soon begin. We skirt Moeraki Point and Moeraki, home of the bizarre circular boulders, and race alongside the open expanses of Katiki Beach and Shag Point, before reaching the town of Palmerston. Beyond Palmerston arguably the most scenic portion of The Southerner route unfolds.

The train climbs spectacularly around the cliffs beyond Karitane, Seacliff and Warrington until, above Blueskin Bay, the line fairly clings

South of Timaru the line hugs the coastline until, at Otaio, it begins creeping inland. The wide Waitaki River bridge at Glenavy is crossed (all 3000 feet of it, making it the second longest rail bridge in New Zealand) before The Southerner meets up with the sea again at Oamaru.

Oamaru has been described as New Zealand's most complete Victorian town, closely resembling an elaborate set for a nineteenth-century film. The old sandstone buildings provide an architectural distinctiveness not found in any other New Zealand town. A day can be spent just roaming around, as the townsfolk go about their everyday activities in a setting that seems inappropriate for cellphones and laptop computers.

The Southerner approaches Shag Point near Palmerston on the journey south. D.L.A. Turner

to the cliff face high above the ocean inlet.

From such a position seascapes dominate with the open ocean providing the bigger picture. Such picturesque aspects of the Otago coast would be missed if you chose to travel by road.

As the train emerges from the Mihiwaka Tunnel and the surrounding hills, the Dunedin suburb of Port Chalmers suddenly appears to the left. These days Port Chalmers, one of the oldest areas of an historic city, functions as a highly specialised container port on Otago Harbour. The glimpses of Port Chalmers with its established villas and the harbour-fringed suburbs of Dunedin, with a look of Victorian permanence about them, remind us that the

The Southerner snakes around Sawyers Bay on the outskirts of Dunedin. Ken Devlin

train will soon be arriving in a city that in many ways has withstood the march of progress – certainly in architectural terms.

Dunedin has, in fact, been described as the cradle of European culture and commerce in New Zealand. Originally settled by Presbyterians of the Free Church of Scotland in 1848, it soon became the wealthiest and most influential New Zealand settlement. The discovery of gold in Central Otago helped fuel Dunedin's development, and wealthy benefactors were able to help establish museums, libraries, art galleries and theatres and the first university and medical school.

The first port of call, Dunedin railway station, is a startling example of the distinctiveness of the city. One of its kind, the station has survived from the early days of rail operation in the area and remains a glowing testament to the skill of its designer, George Troup.

A fascinating option available to Southerner passengers is the "Queenstown Connection", incorporating the train fare from Christchurch to Dunedin. On reaching this Edinburgh of the south (the train arrives just before 2pm), several hours at leisure are available to lose yourself in the city's old-world character. If you've never been to Dunedin before, the glimpses of yesteryear, plethora of restored villas and magnificent old churches will in itself make the journey worthwhile.

Optional activities on day two include

The Southerner continuing south through coastal cattle country in the Seacliff area with the South Pacific Ocean in the background. Ken Devlin

visiting historic Olveston House, Speights Brewery and Larnach Castle on the Otago Peninsula, before catching the afternoon train plying the Taieri Gorge Railway. This faithfully restored excursion train has become a genuine visitor attraction.

A trip on the Taieri Gorge Railway is a must for all train buffs, not just those hooking into the "Queenstown Connection". For those who mourned the closure of the Central Otago line from Cromwell to Dunedin, the re-emergence of the Taieri Gorge Railway has provided considerable compensation. Admittedly the excursion train only goes as far as Pukerangi, but there remain hopes that one day considerably more of the old line will be restored. As it is, the branch that swings away from the main line at Wingatui takes the striking-looking train (bright yellow carriages with white roofs and dark brown edgings) through some of the most ruggedly handsome scenery in New Zealand. The Taieri Gorge is a spectacular lunar landscape with yawning viaducts and precipitous cliffs. Unlike any other train journey in New Zealand, it remains the classic example of the way many train routes take you where the roads can't. No one in their right mind would try to construct a road through the Taieri Gorge.

From Pukerangi a coach completes the "Queenstown Connection". Within easy range of Queenstown another restored excursion train awaits rail enthusiasts and visitors in general: "The Kingston Flyer", a faithful replica of the original steam train that, decades earlier, plied the track from the deep south all the way to Kingston at the southern end of Lake Wakatipu. In conjunction with the Taieri Gorge Railway, The Kingston Flyer represents a heady dose of railway nostalgia.

The Kingston Flyer operation is made up of two lovingly restored Ab steam engines and seven wooden carriages. There is even a turn-of-the-century buffet car featuring native New Zealand wood panelling and fixtures, together with an authentic 1898 "Birdcage" compartment car. Although The Flyer only travels as far south as Fairlight these days, a half-hour jaunt, its uniqueness and unlikely setting in the middle of nowhere make for a memorable experience. The Flyer can also be hired for special celebrations, and "hold-ups" of the train, redolent of wild west days, can be arranged for those wishing to relive a slice of history.

For those travellers wishing to stay within Dunedin and its immediate environs, a harbour cruise on the award-winning *Monarch* is a pleasant way to spend a few hours between trains. The unique and unusual wildlife at the head of the peninsula includes albatross, yellow-eyed penguin and seal colonies. The yellow-eyed penguin is the rarest in the world, and the albatross colony is the world's only mainland colony of this majestic bird.

The Southerner departs from Dunedin in the early afternoon, and before long the southern suburbs with their continuing rows of villas and Victorian era buildings remind you of the area's heritage. Carisbrook, home of Otago rugby and cricket, is skirted on an embankment that used to double as a long-range grandstand in days when famous sporting events were being staged. It was also a reminder of the Scottish heritage of Dunedin – no sense paying to see what you could see for free.

Mosgiel, with its woollen mills, is the first stop on this "deeper south" stretch, and soon The Southerner is pounding a beat across the Taieri Plains, the Taieri River and past the still waters of Lake Waihola, before reaching Milton just before 3pm. Just south of here, at Clarksville Junction, the long Roxburgh branch line used to head inland. Had the Roxburgh link continued a few miles further it would have connected up with the Central Otago line at Alexandra. Nostalgia buffs still drool about the possibilities such an inland umbilicus would have allowed: the definitive round trip that would have provided a scenic smorgasbord.

The Clutha River, one of the mightiest in New Zealand, is crossed in spectacular fashion at Balclutha, before discharging into the Pacific Ocean a few miles to the east. By now The Southerner is heading due west as it crosses the rolling hills of Southland, before pulling into Gore at 4.21pm. Gore is known as the brown trout capital and the home of New Zealand country music.

The light begins to fade as we become aware of the fact that we are approaching the end of the line – in every sense. The line at Gore suddenly heads due south, through Mataura with its large pulp and paper mill, until at Edendale, on the Southland Plains, it makes its final south-west approach to Invercargill.

At 5.15pm we finally reach New Zealand's southernmost city. Not only does The Southerner terminate here, but the stop represents the southernmost reach of Tranz Scenic's passenger services. There are doubts that this is the southernmost passenger service in the world, but there are just as many travellers prepared to swear that this is indeed the case. Perhaps the Patagonian Daylight in South America has stronger claims to such status, but it will take a careful examination of a world atlas to settle the argument.

By any account there is a feeling of accomplishment as The Southerner disgorges its load at Invercargill station and an icy wind blasts up from the "deepest south". Passenger trains used to run further south to the port of Bluff, but right now Invercargill is very much the end of the line.

On 8 August 1863 a locomotive called Lady Barkly ran on a short line of wooden rails on Invercargill wharf, the first time a steam locomotive had operated over any stretch of track in New Zealand. Such knowledge enhances the ancient status, by New Zealand measures, of the city of Invercargill, which is not only one of the southernmost cities in the world but, because of its many historic buildings from the late nineteenth century, also ranks as one of New Zealand's oldest.

The stuttering exploits of the Lady Barkly along the Invercargill wharf and the 589 kilometres of The Southerner route provide a stark contrast. There is also a lingering feeling of disappointment that, for admittedly very sound geographical reasons, the line ends here.

Above: *The splendid railway station at Dunedin built in 1906 of basalt and limestone.* Ken Devlin

My Paper Folding Easy Origami

1

Basics of Paper Folding
Follow the instructions carefully before you start paper folding.

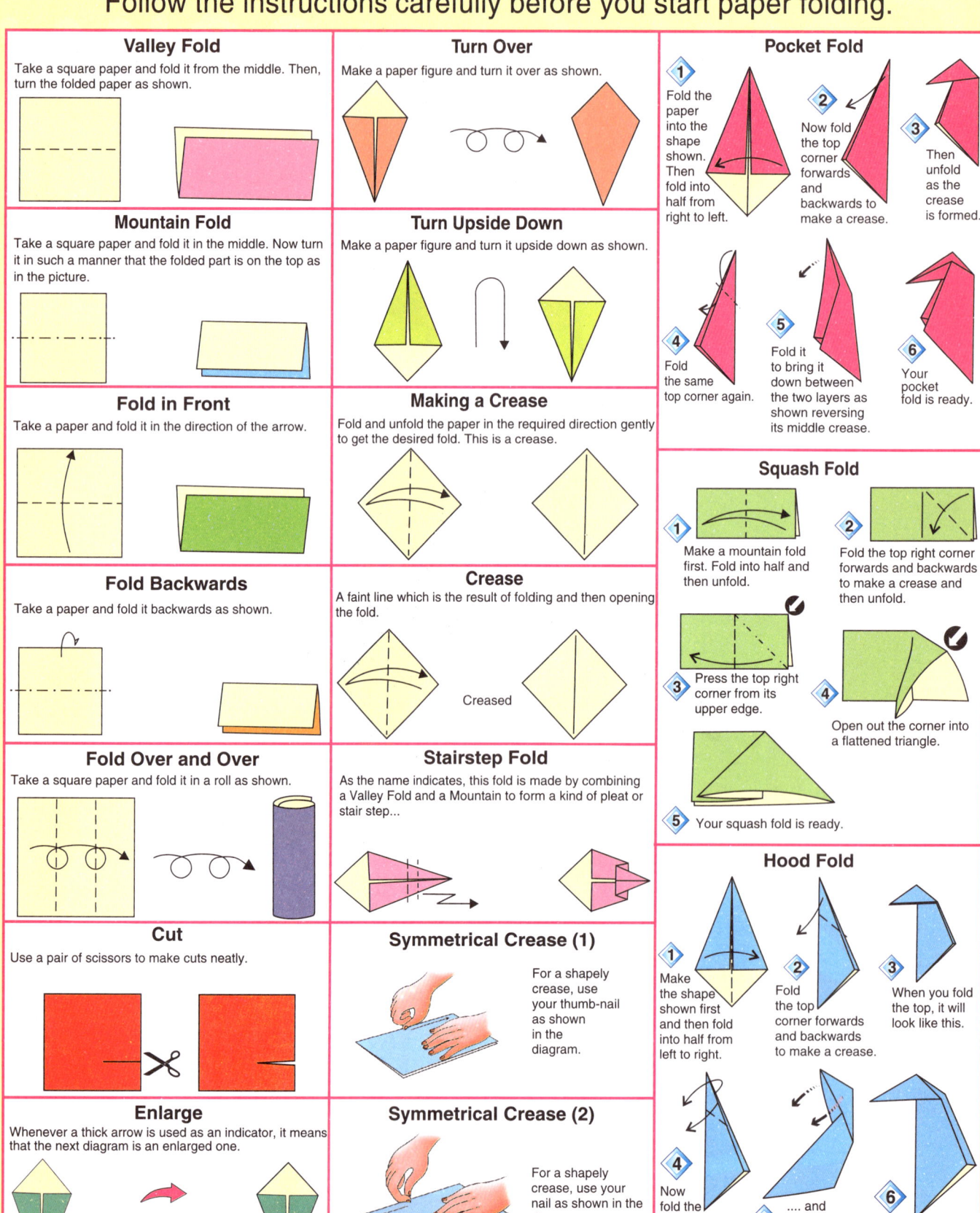

Valley Fold
Take a square paper and fold it from the middle. Then, turn the folded paper as shown.

Mountain Fold
Take a square paper and fold it in the middle. Now turn it in such a manner that the folded part is on the top as in the picture.

Fold in Front
Take a paper and fold it in the direction of the arrow.

Fold Backwards
Take a paper and fold it backwards as shown.

Fold Over and Over
Take a square paper and fold it in a roll as shown.

Cut
Use a pair of scissors to make cuts neatly.

Enlarge
Whenever a thick arrow is used as an indicator, it means that the next diagram is an enlarged one.

a swollen arrow

Turn Over
Make a paper figure and turn it over as shown.

Turn Upside Down
Make a paper figure and turn it upside down as shown.

Making a Crease
Fold and unfold the paper in the required direction gently to get the desired fold. This is a crease.

Crease
A faint line which is the result of folding and then opening the fold.

Creased

Stairstep Fold
As the name indicates, this fold is made by combining a Valley Fold and a Mountain to form a kind of pleat or stair step...

Symmetrical Crease (1)
For a shapely crease, use your thumb-nail as shown in the diagram.

Symmetrical Crease (2)
For a shapely crease, use your nail as shown in the diagram.

Pocket Fold
1. Fold the paper into the shape shown. Then fold into half from right to left.
2. Now fold the top corner forwards and backwards to make a crease.
3. Then unfold as the crease is formed.
4. Fold the same top corner again.
5. Fold it to bring it down between the two layers as shown reversing its middle crease.
6. Your pocket fold is ready.

Squash Fold
1. Make a mountain fold first. Fold into half and then unfold.
2. Fold the top right corner forwards and backwards to make a crease and then unfold.
3. Press the top right corner from its upper edge.
4. Open out the corner into a flattened triangle.
5. Your squash fold is ready.

Hood Fold
1. Make the shape shown first and then fold into half from left to right.
2. Fold the top corner forwards and backwards to make a crease.
3. When you fold the top, it will look like this.
4. Now fold the top corner at the crease inside out...
5. .... and reverse its middle.
6. Your hood fold is ready.

Joker

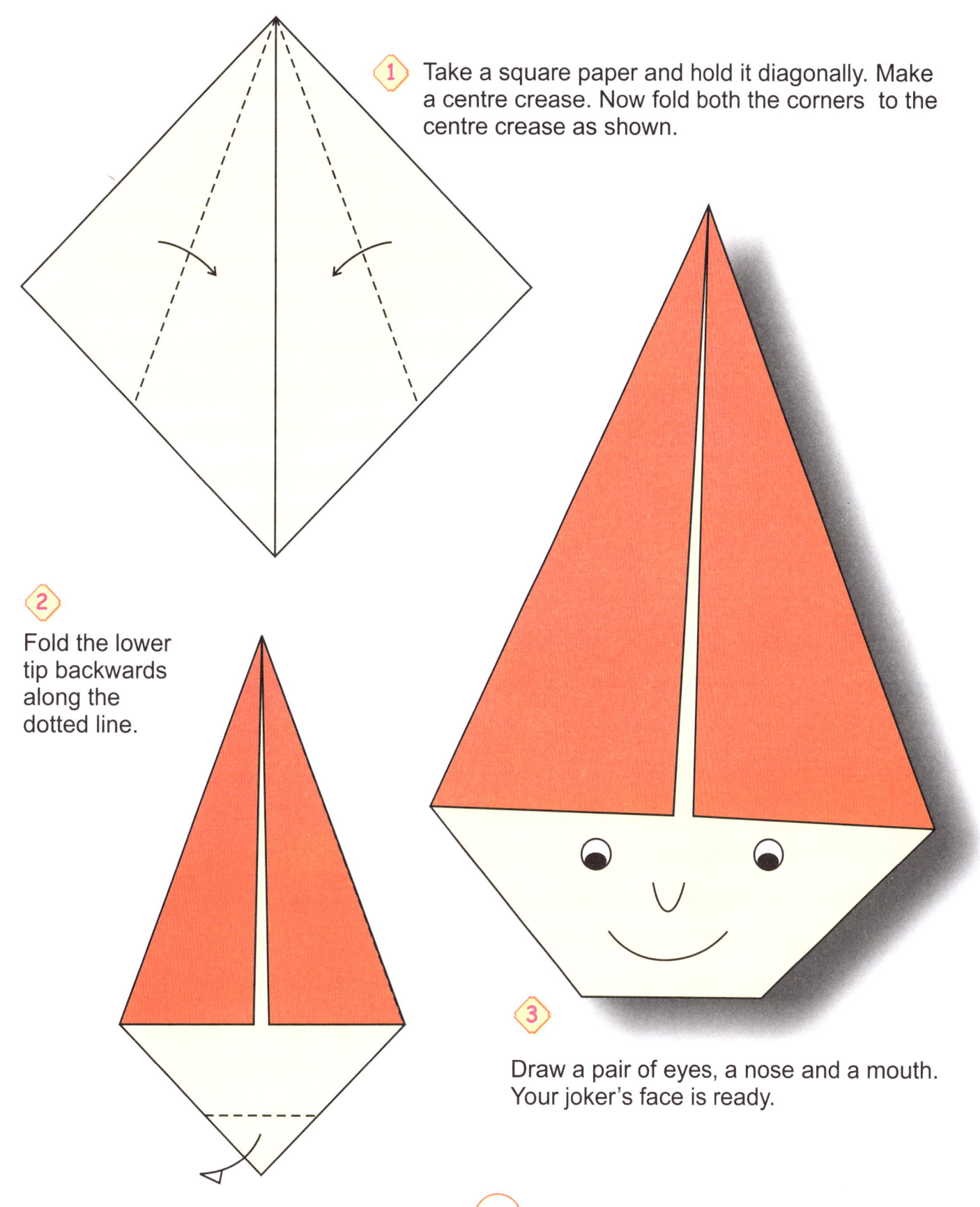

1. Take a square paper and hold it diagonally. Make a centre crease. Now fold both the corners to the centre crease as shown.

2. Fold the lower tip backwards along the dotted line.

3. Draw a pair of eyes, a nose and a mouth. Your joker's face is ready.

Pencil Holder

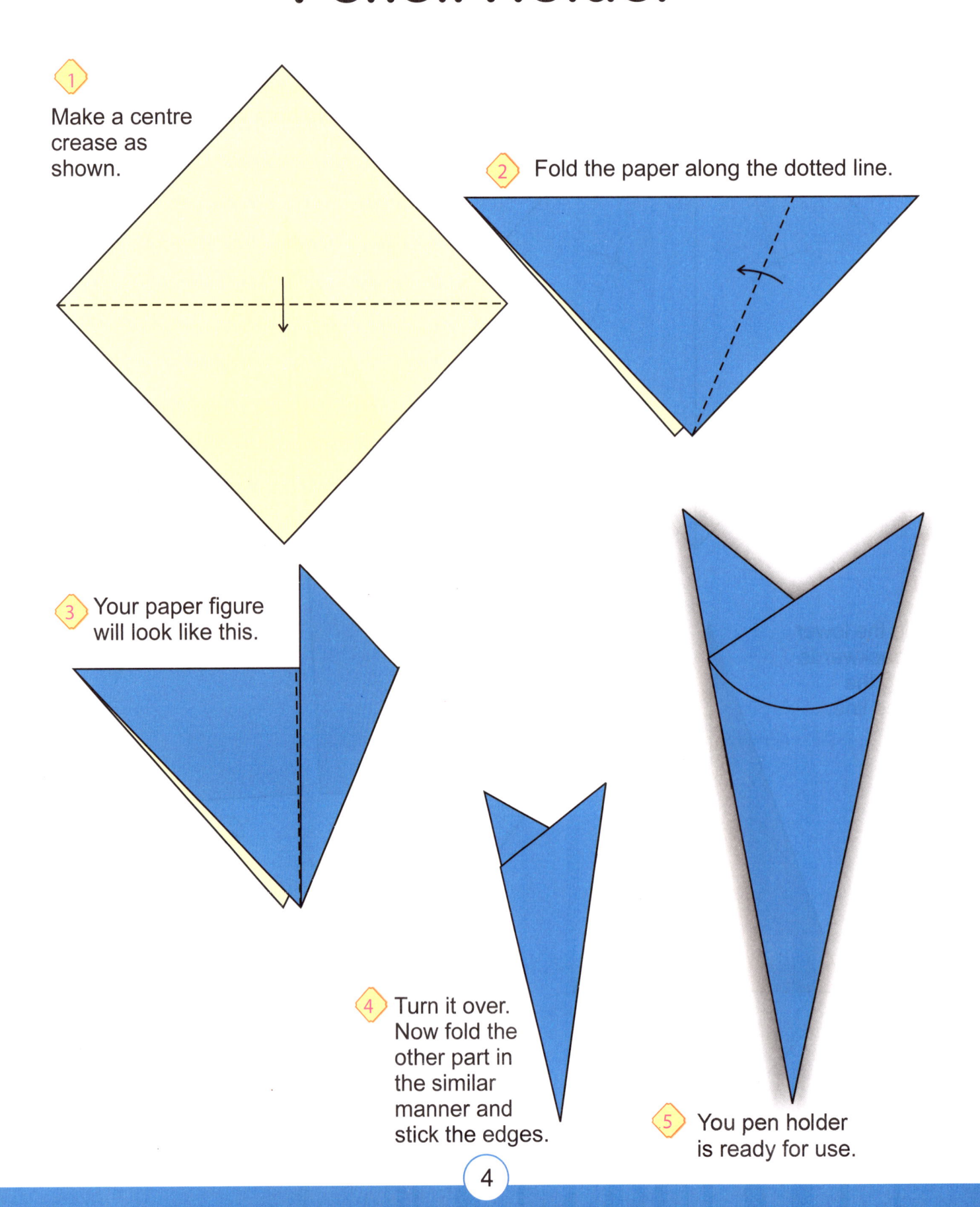

1. Make a centre crease as shown.

2. Fold the paper along the dotted line.

3. Your paper figure will look like this.

4. Turn it over. Now fold the other part in the similar manner and stick the edges.

5. You pen holder is ready for use.

Envelope

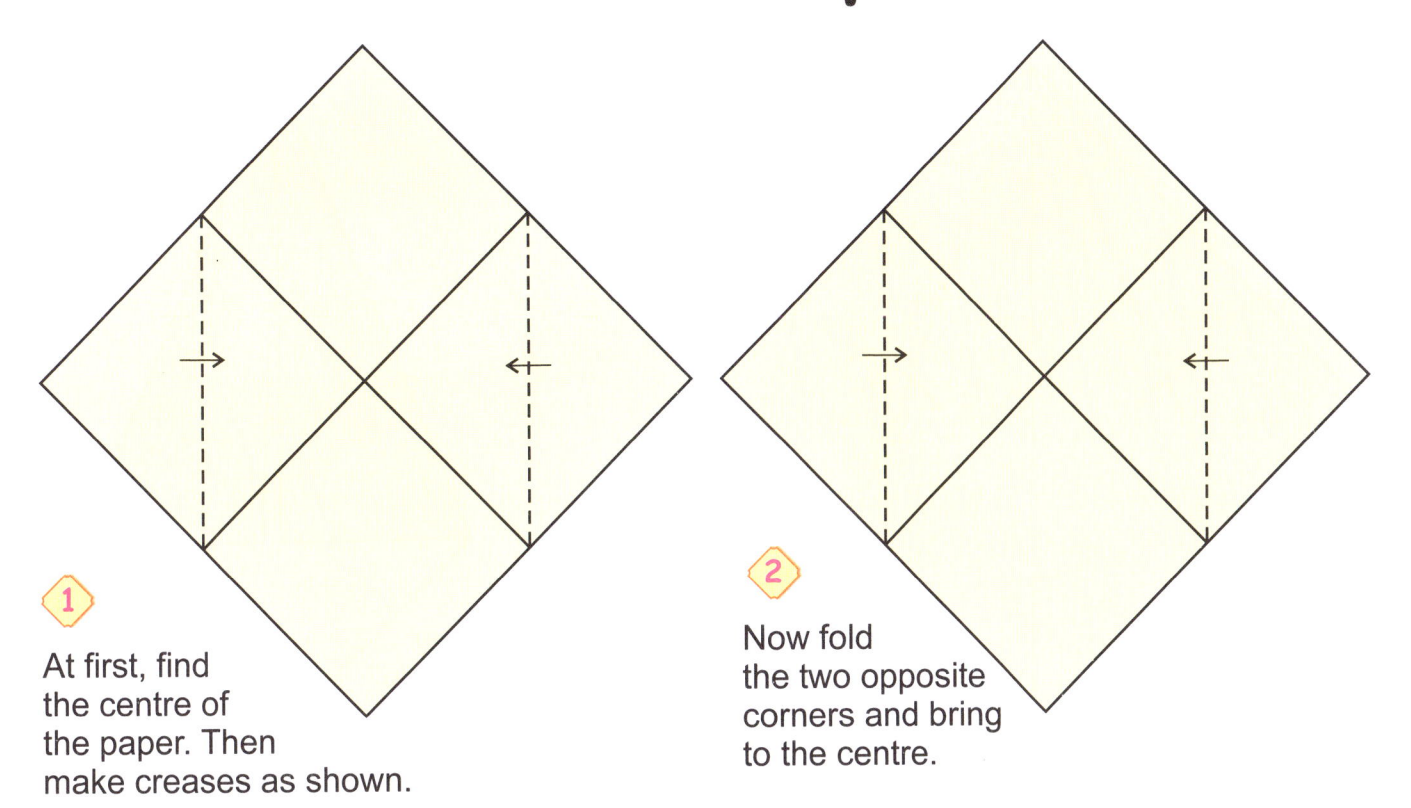

1 At first, find the centre of the paper. Then make creases as shown.

2 Now fold the two opposite corners and bring to the centre.

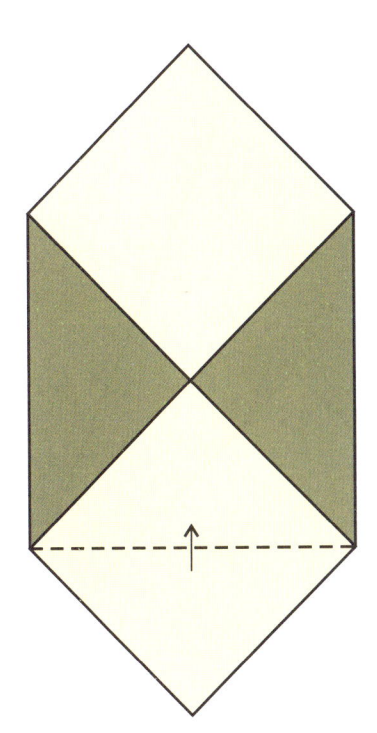

3 Stick the lower corners to the centre with the help of glue. (Leave the upper corner free.)

4 Your envelope is ready to be used.

Hat

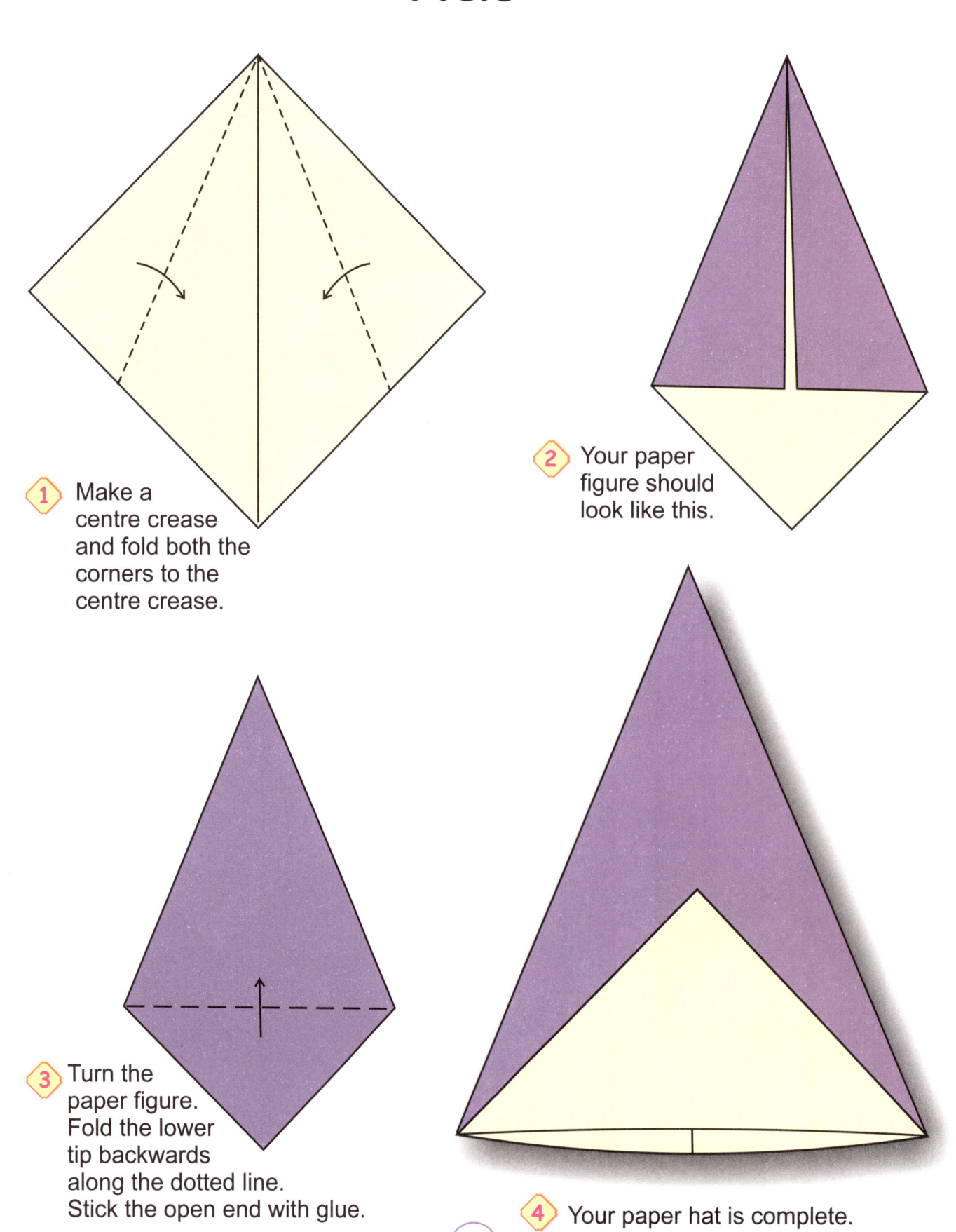

1. Make a centre crease and fold both the corners to the centre crease.

2. Your paper figure should look like this.

3. Turn the paper figure. Fold the lower tip backwards along the dotted line. Stick the open end with glue.

4. Your paper hat is complete.

Cup

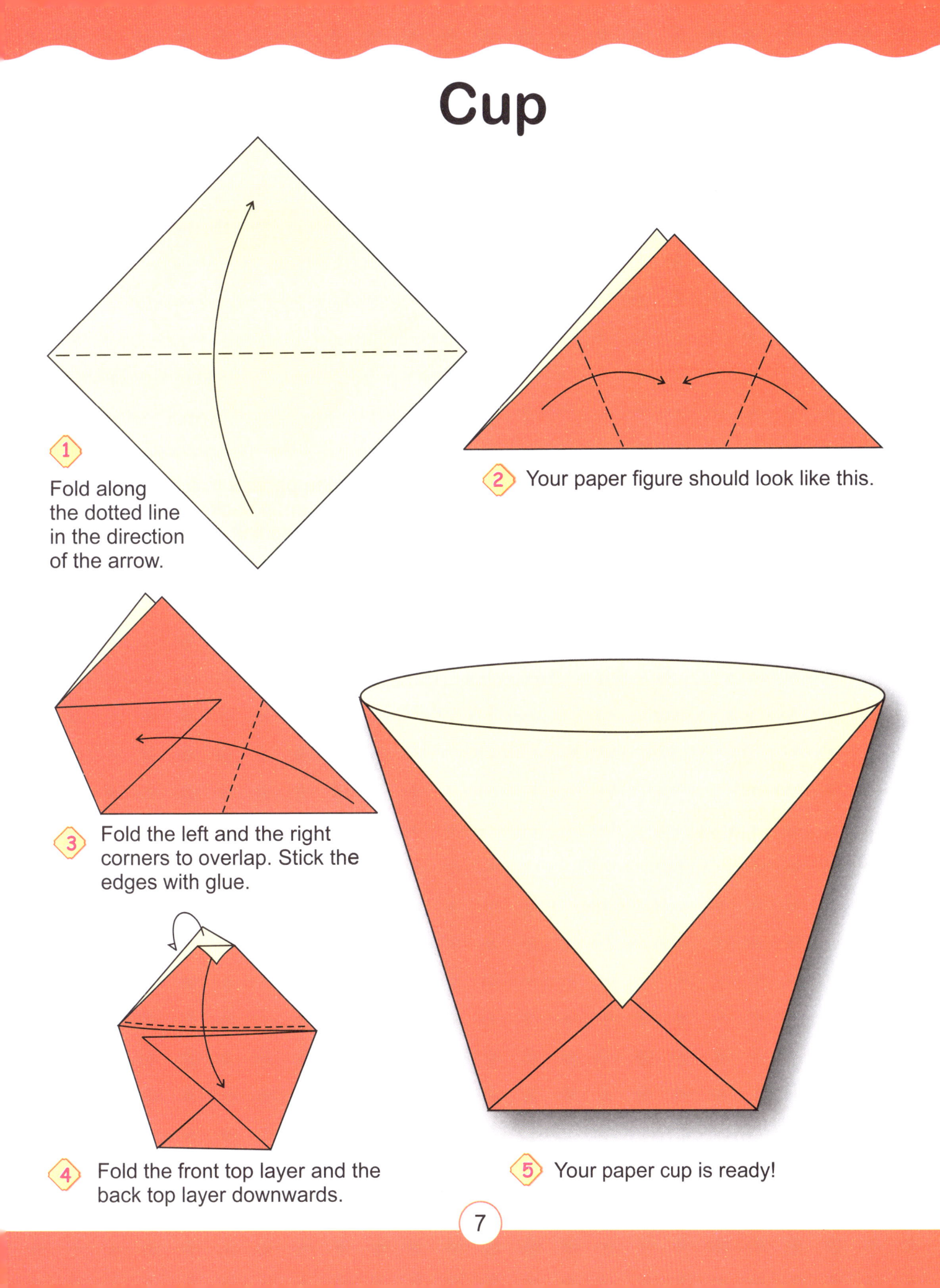

1. Fold along the dotted line in the direction of the arrow.

2. Your paper figure should look like this.

3. Fold the left and the right corners to overlap. Stick the edges with glue.

4. Fold the front top layer and the back top layer downwards.

5. Your paper cup is ready!

Bird

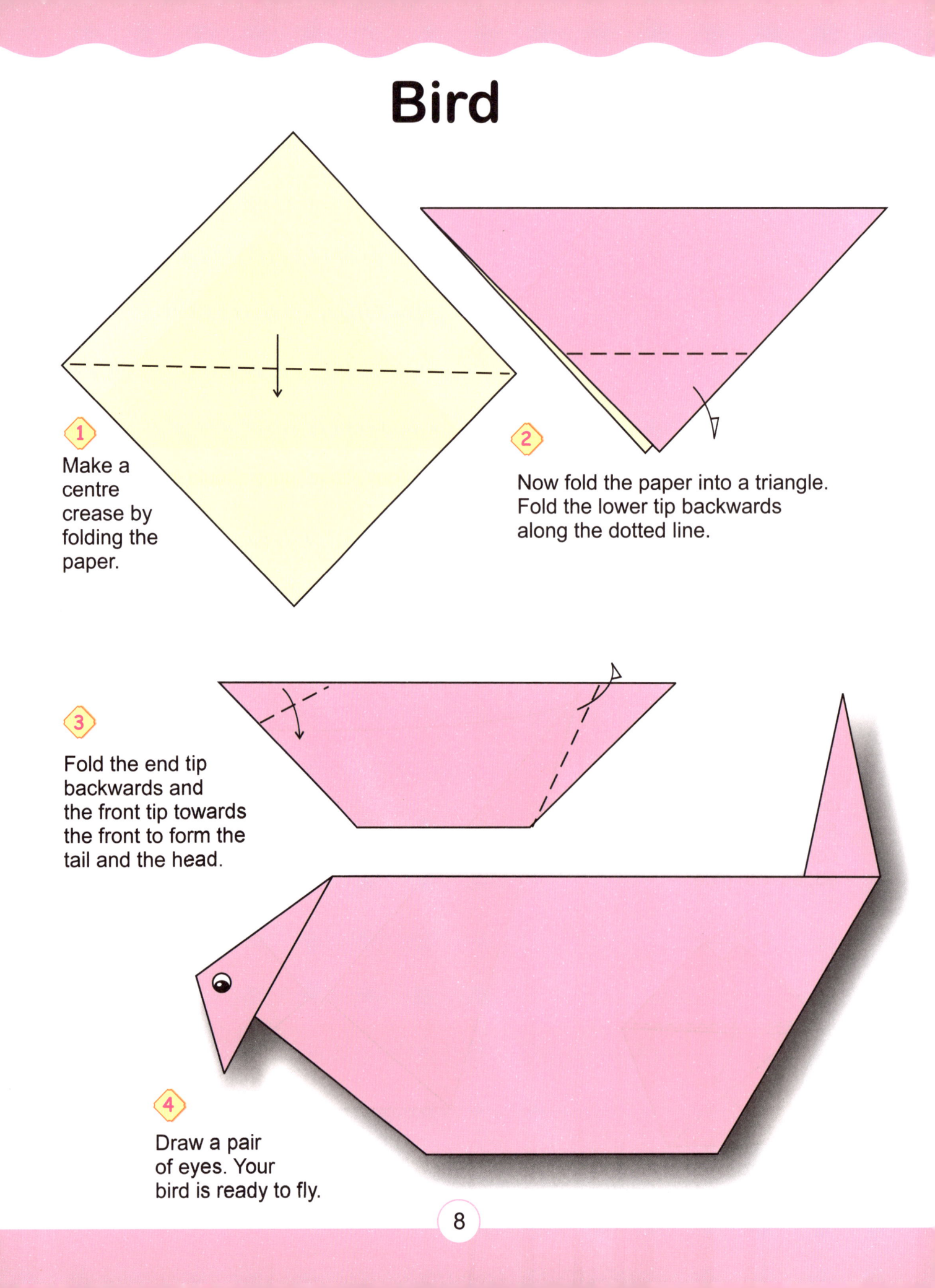

1 Make a centre crease by folding the paper.

2 Now fold the paper into a triangle. Fold the lower tip backwards along the dotted line.

3 Fold the end tip backwards and the front tip towards the front to form the tail and the head.

4 Draw a pair of eyes. Your bird is ready to fly.

House

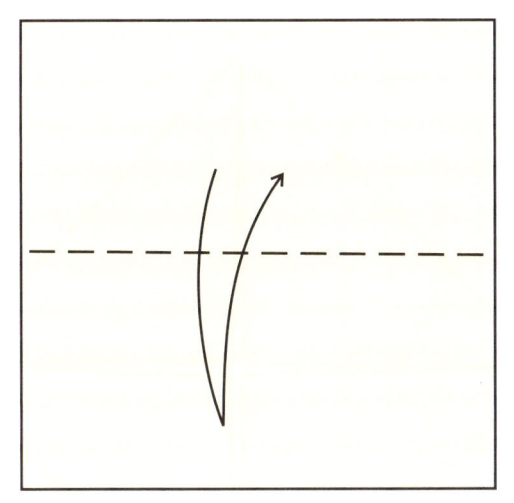

1. Fold and unfold along the dotted line to make a centre crease.

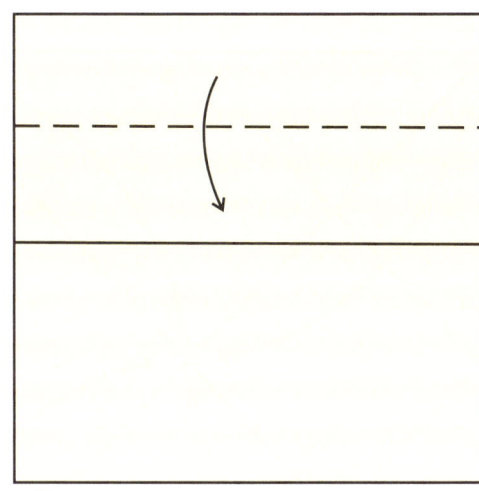

2. Fold the top flap along the dotted lines to the centre crease.

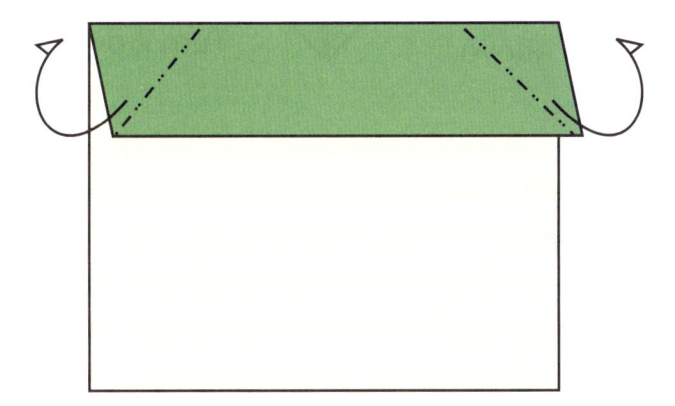

3. Fold the two corners behind along the dotted lines.

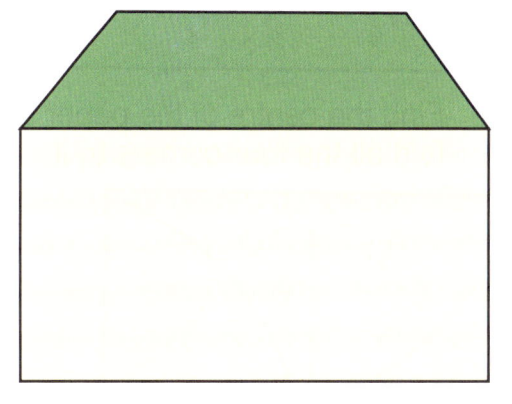

4. Your paper house should look the this.

5. Now draw the door and the windows. Your pretty paper house is ready.

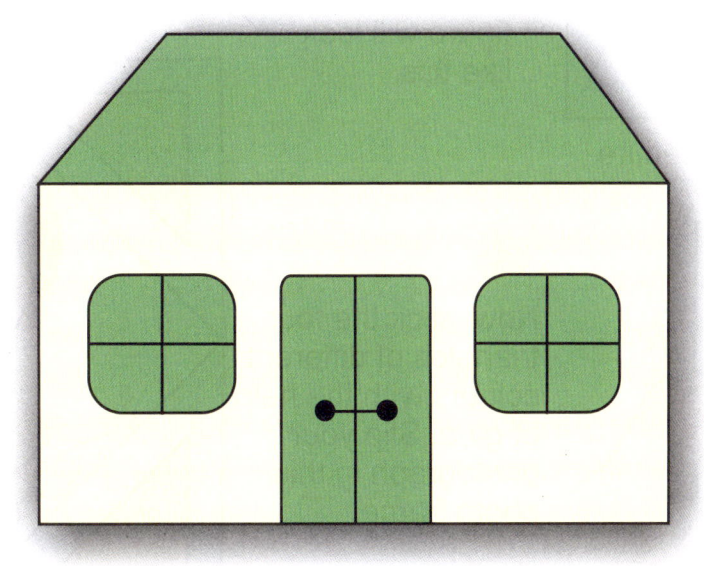

Photo Frame

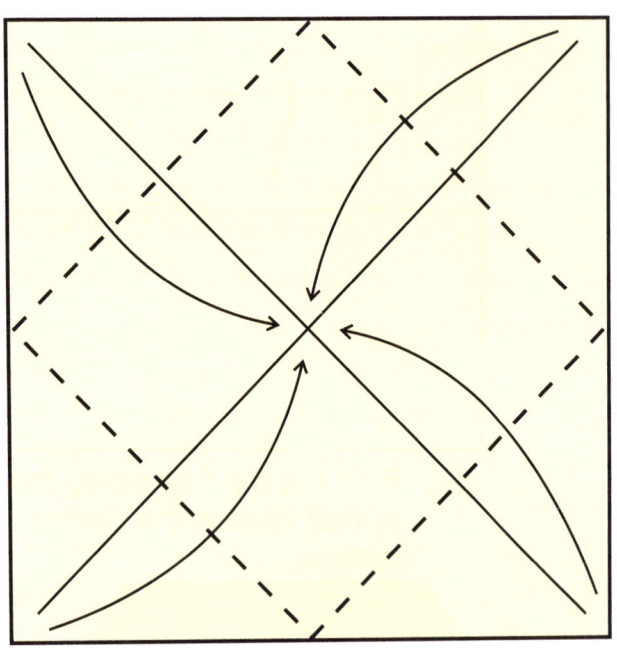

1. Find the centre of the paper and fold all the four corners to it.

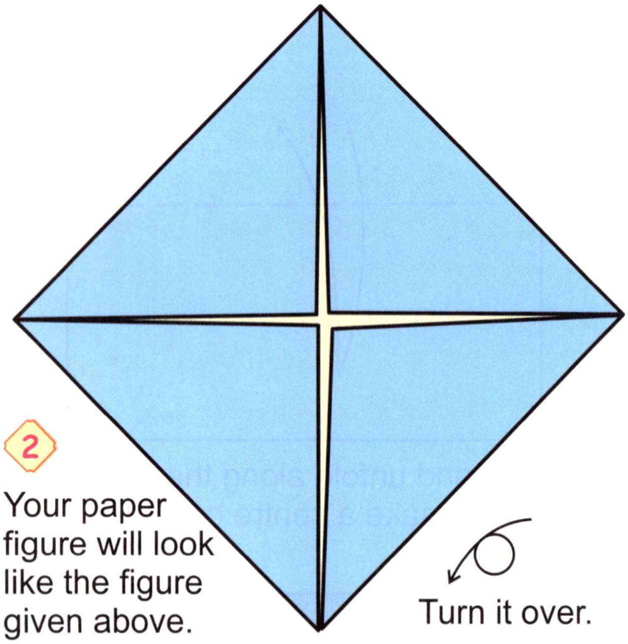

2. Your paper figure will look like the figure given above. Turn it over.

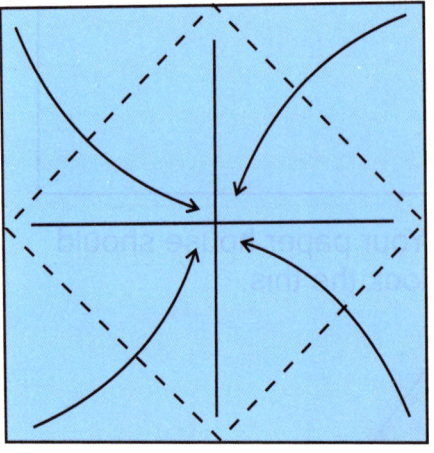

3. Repeat the procedure as in step 1.

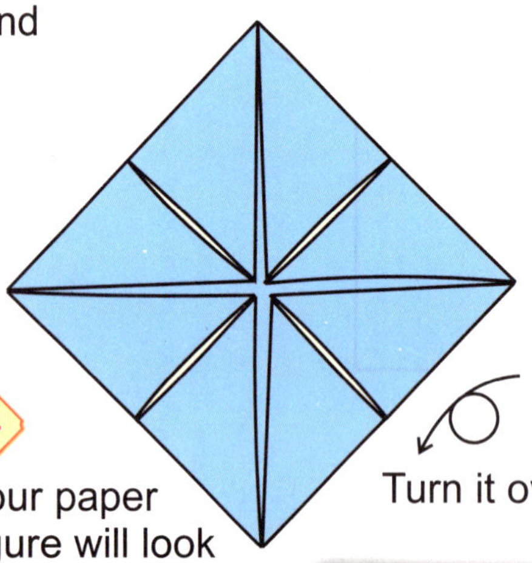

4. Your paper figure will look like this. Turn it over.

5. Turn all the four flaps inwards and crease neatly.

6. Now, stick the four triangles of different colours with the help of glue. Slip your photograph in this photo frame.

10

Owl

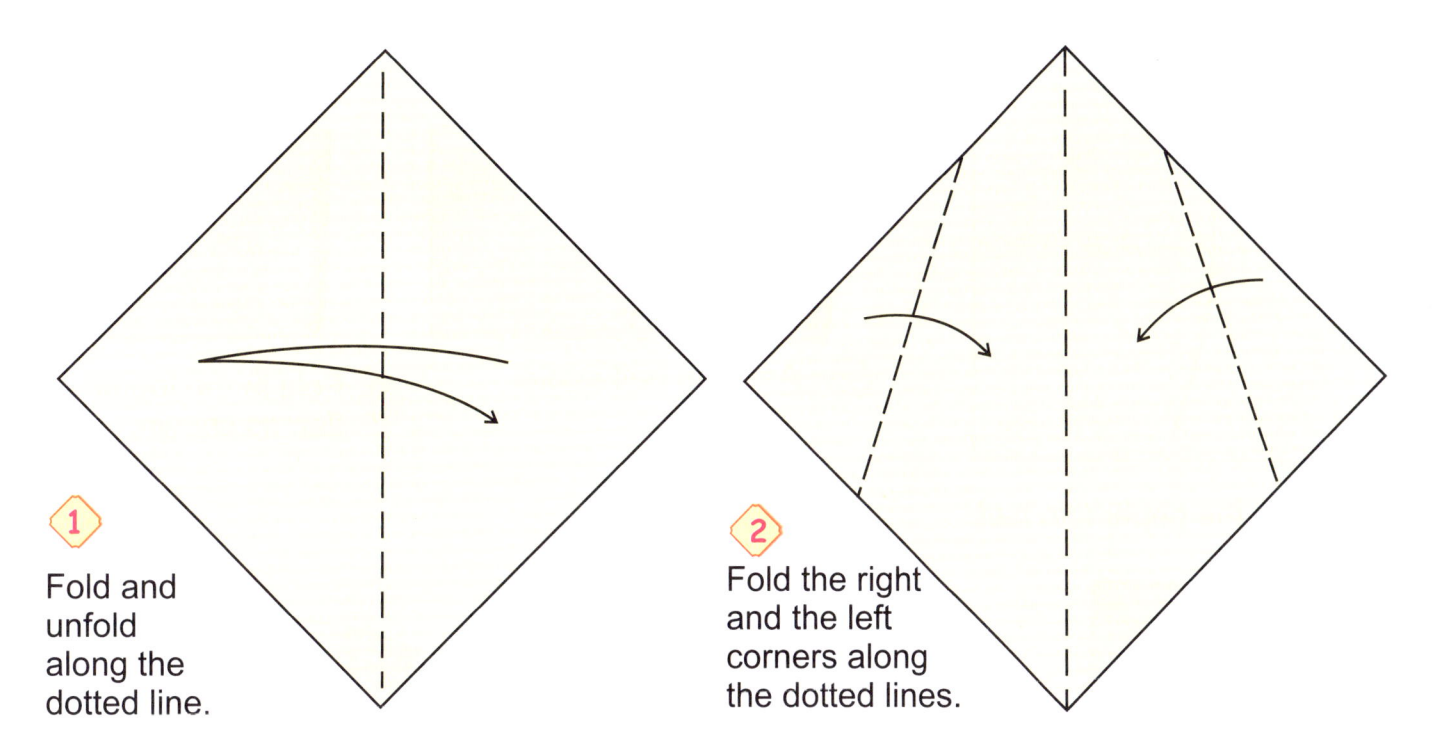

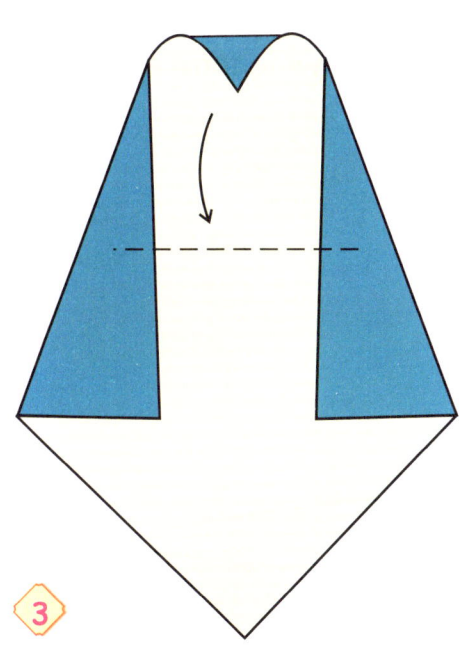

① Fold and unfold along the dotted line.

② Fold the right and the left corners along the dotted lines.

③ Fold the top corner downward along the dotted line to make the head of the owl.

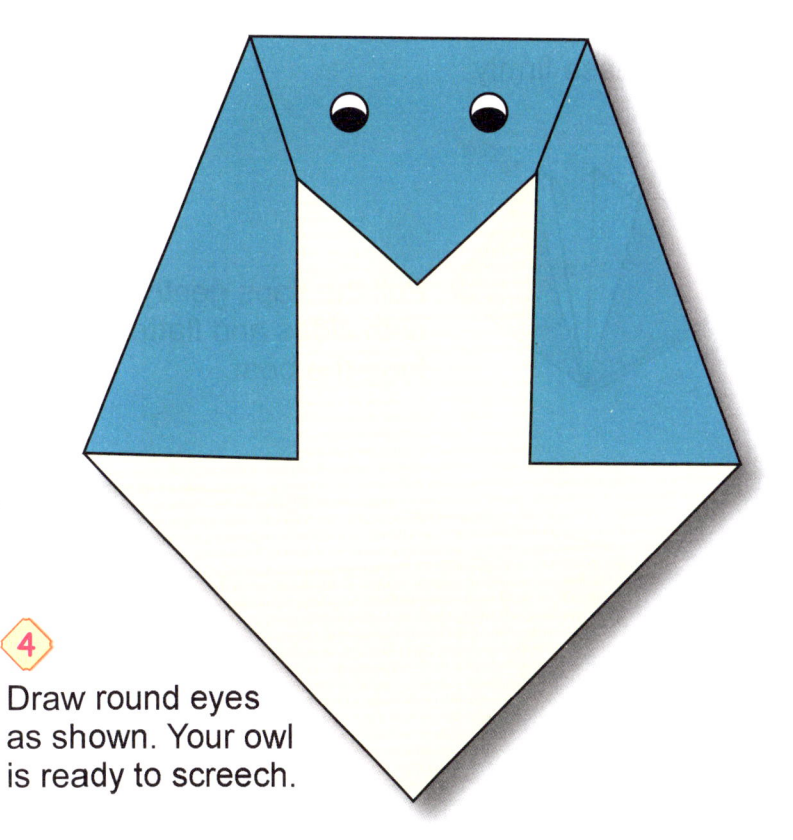

④ Draw round eyes as shown. Your owl is ready to screech.

Boat

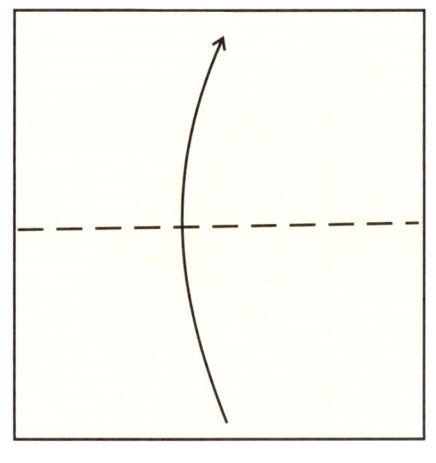

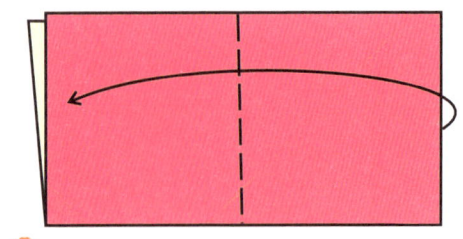

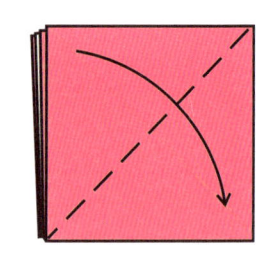

1. Fold the paper into half.

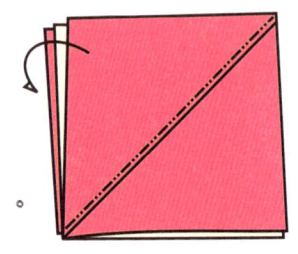

2. And into half again.

3. Fold in the topmost flap as shown.

4. And the other three flaps backwards and crease firmly.

5. Your paper figure should look like this.

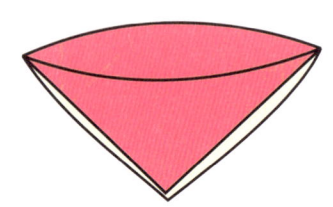

6. Insert your thumbs in and open out the model and flatten it to form a square.

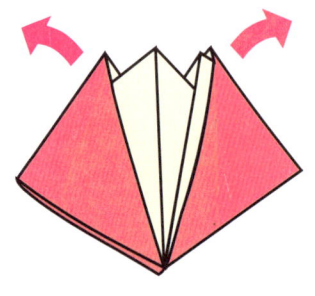

7. Pull the flaps gently from both sides and flatten to form the boat.

8. Your boat is ready to sail.

12

Mouse

1. Make a centre crease and unfold.

2. Fold the top and the bottom corner upto the centre crease.

3. Fold the lower corner inwards along the dotted line.

4. Now fold into half along the dotted line.

5. Your paper figure should look like this.

6. Cut two small round pieces of a different coloured paper for the ears.

7. Stick the ears on the head as shown. Do stick a long, thin strip at the back to make the tail. Your mouse is ready to squeak.

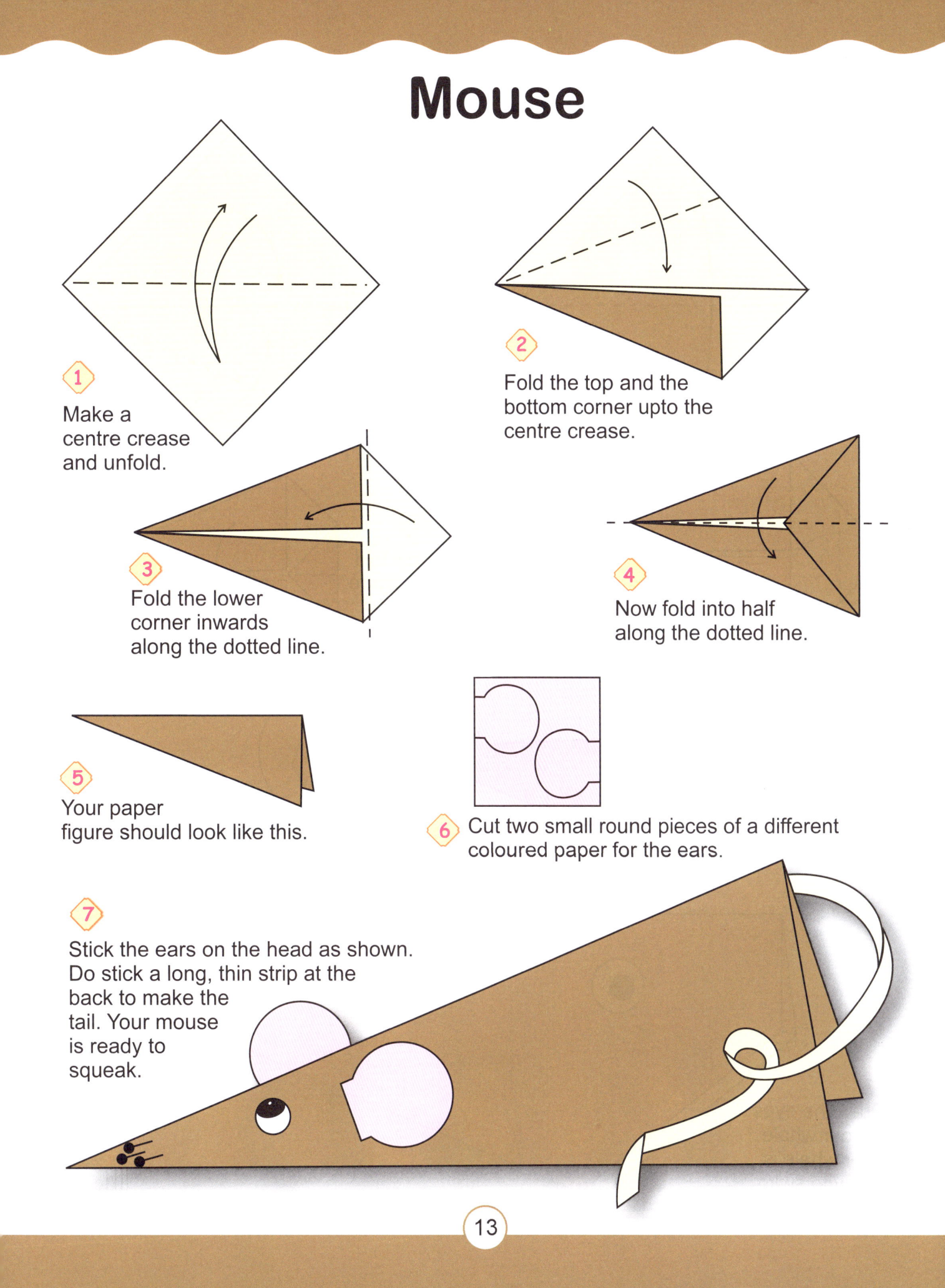

Whale

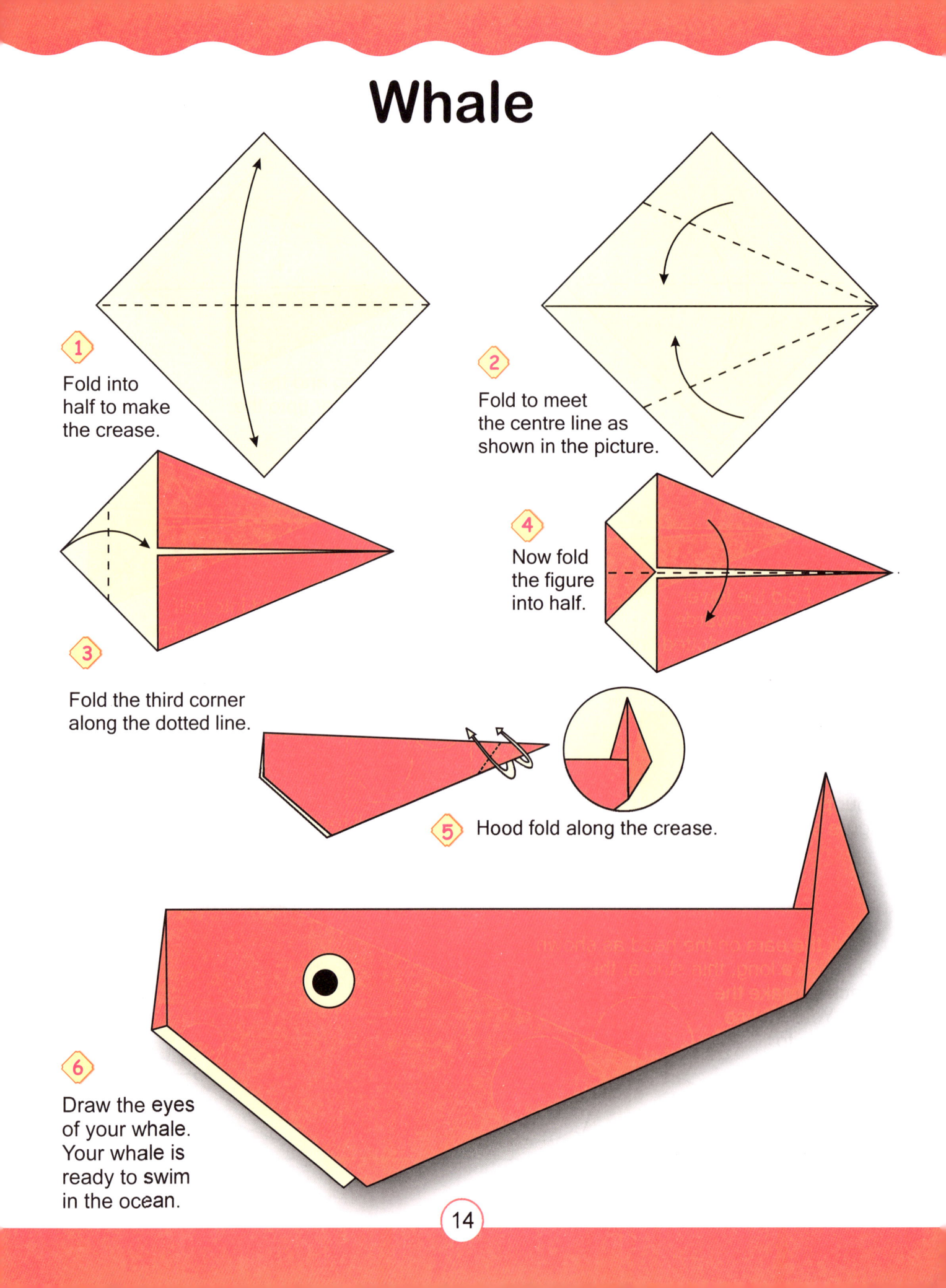

1. Fold into half to make the crease.

2. Fold to meet the centre line as shown in the picture.

3. Fold the third corner along the dotted line.

4. Now fold the figure into half.

5. Hood fold along the crease.

6. Draw the eyes of your whale. Your whale is ready to swim in the ocean.

Aeroplane

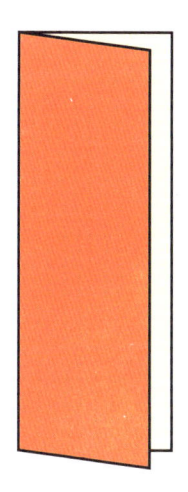

1 Fold an 8½ ×11 cm piece of paper into half, horizontally.

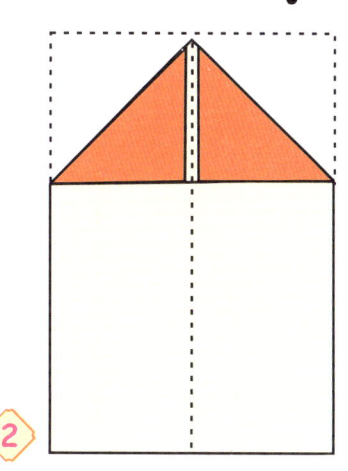

2 Unfold the paper, then fold the top two corners down to the centre of the paper to form a triangle.

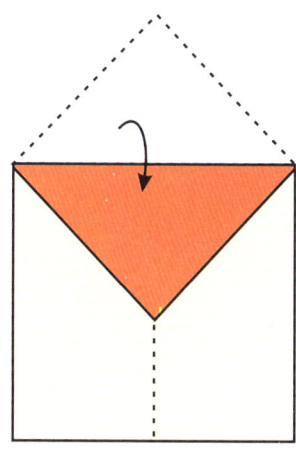

3 Fold down the top to form a triangle.

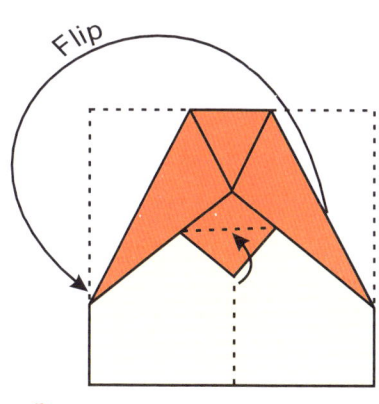

4 Fold the top two corners down until the corners meet each other at a point. Now fold the lower tip along the dotted line.

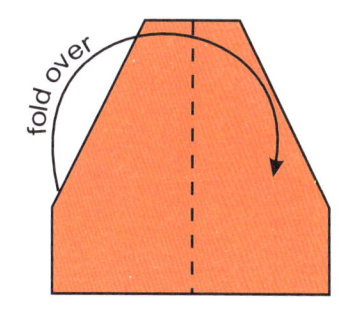

5 Now turn the paper figure and fold it into half lengthwise.

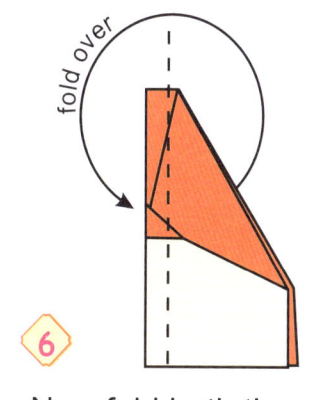

6 Now fold both the sides, one towards the back and the other towards the front to form the wings.

7 Your aeroplane is ready to fly.

Shirt

1. Take a rectangular piece of paper.

2. Fold it backwards along the upper dotted line.

3. Cut the paper as shown in the figure.

4. Fold along the dotted line in the direction of the arrow.

5. Fold the upper and lower corners backwards along the dotted lines.

6. Fold the lower layer backwards along the dotted line.

7. Your shirt is ready to be worn.

16

Jet

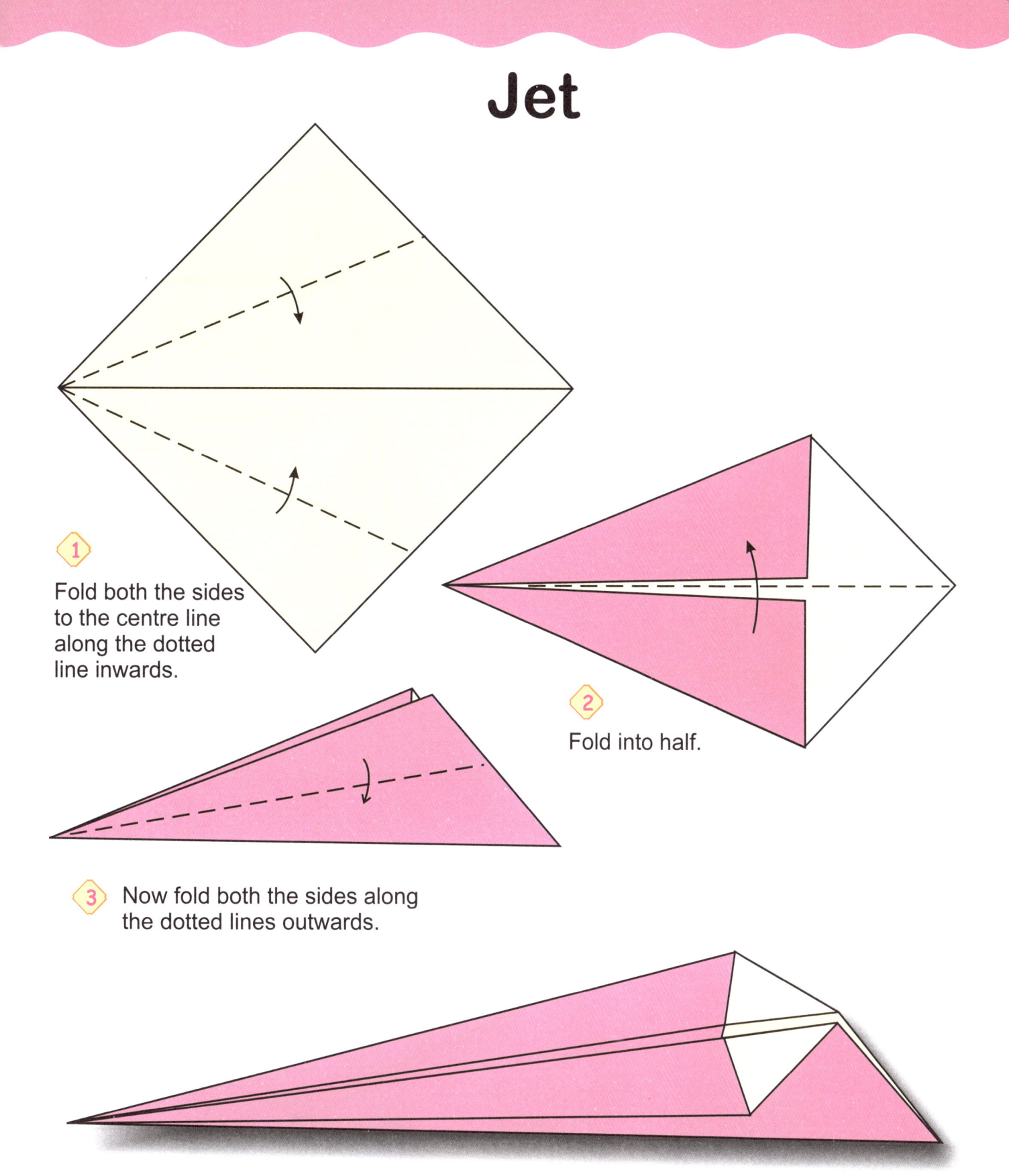

1. Fold both the sides to the centre line along the dotted line inwards.

2. Fold into half.

3. Now fold both the sides along the dotted lines outwards.

4. Your paper figure will look like this. Fold along the dotted line and your jet is ready to take off.

Star

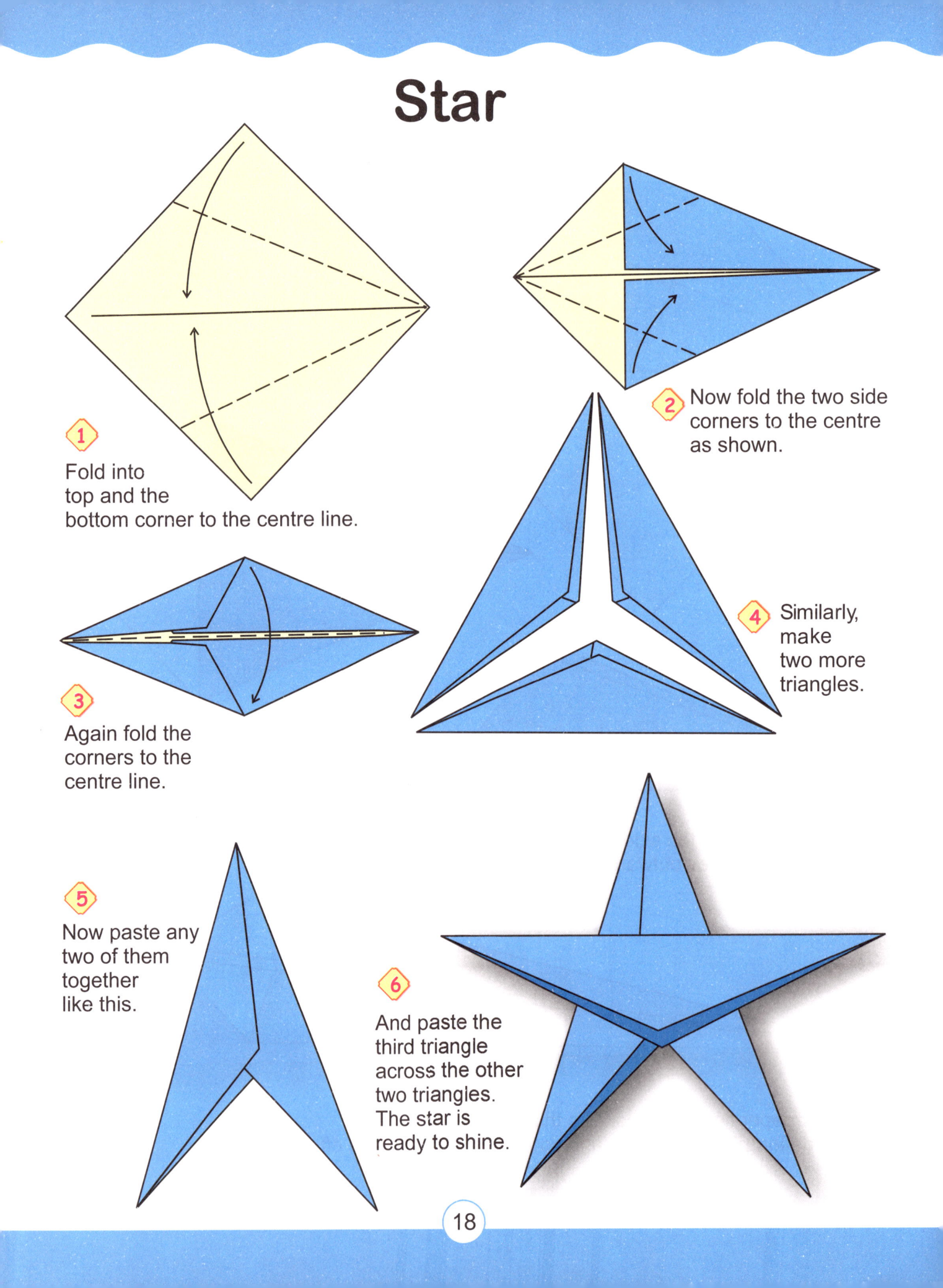

1. Fold into top and the bottom corner to the centre line.

2. Now fold the two side corners to the centre as shown.

3. Again fold the corners to the centre line.

4. Similarly, make two more triangles.

5. Now paste any two of them together like this.

6. And paste the third triangle across the other two triangles. The star is ready to shine.

Table

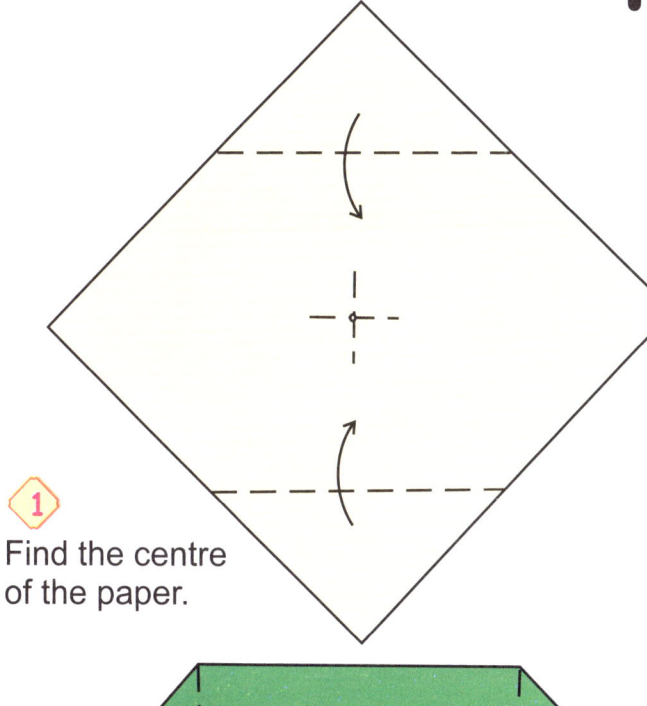

1. Find the centre of the paper.

2. Now fold the 2 opposite corners and stick them to the crntre.

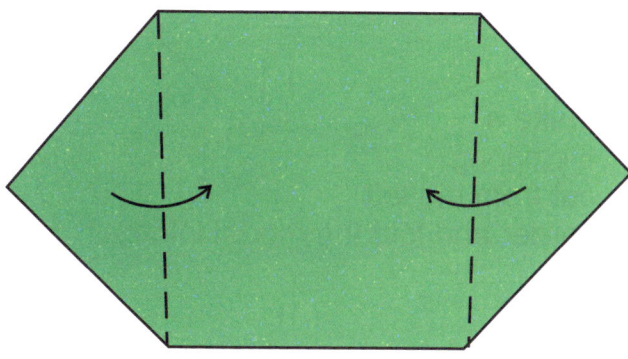

3. Turn it over after folding.

4. Now fold each corner from the creases to the centre.

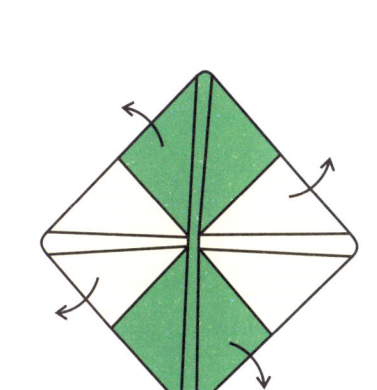

5. Pull out all the four sides outwards to make the 4 legs of the table on which it will stand.

6. Your cute little paper table is ready.

19

Bunny Rabbit

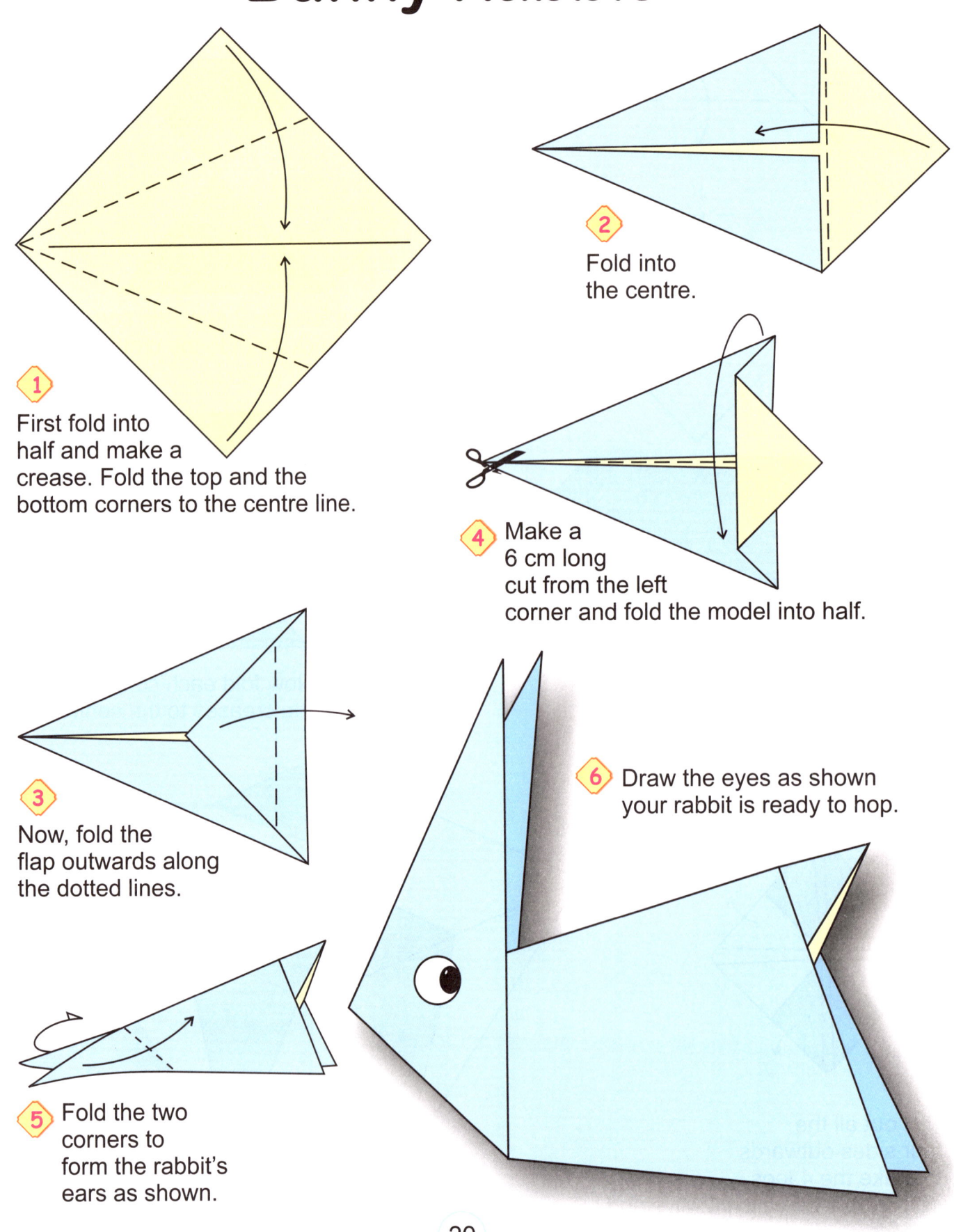

1 First fold into half and make a crease. Fold the top and the bottom corners to the centre line.

2 Fold into the centre.

3 Now, fold the flap outwards along the dotted lines.

4 Make a 6 cm long cut from the left corner and fold the model into half.

5 Fold the two corners to form the rabbit's ears as shown.

6 Draw the eyes as shown your rabbit is ready to hop.

Peacock

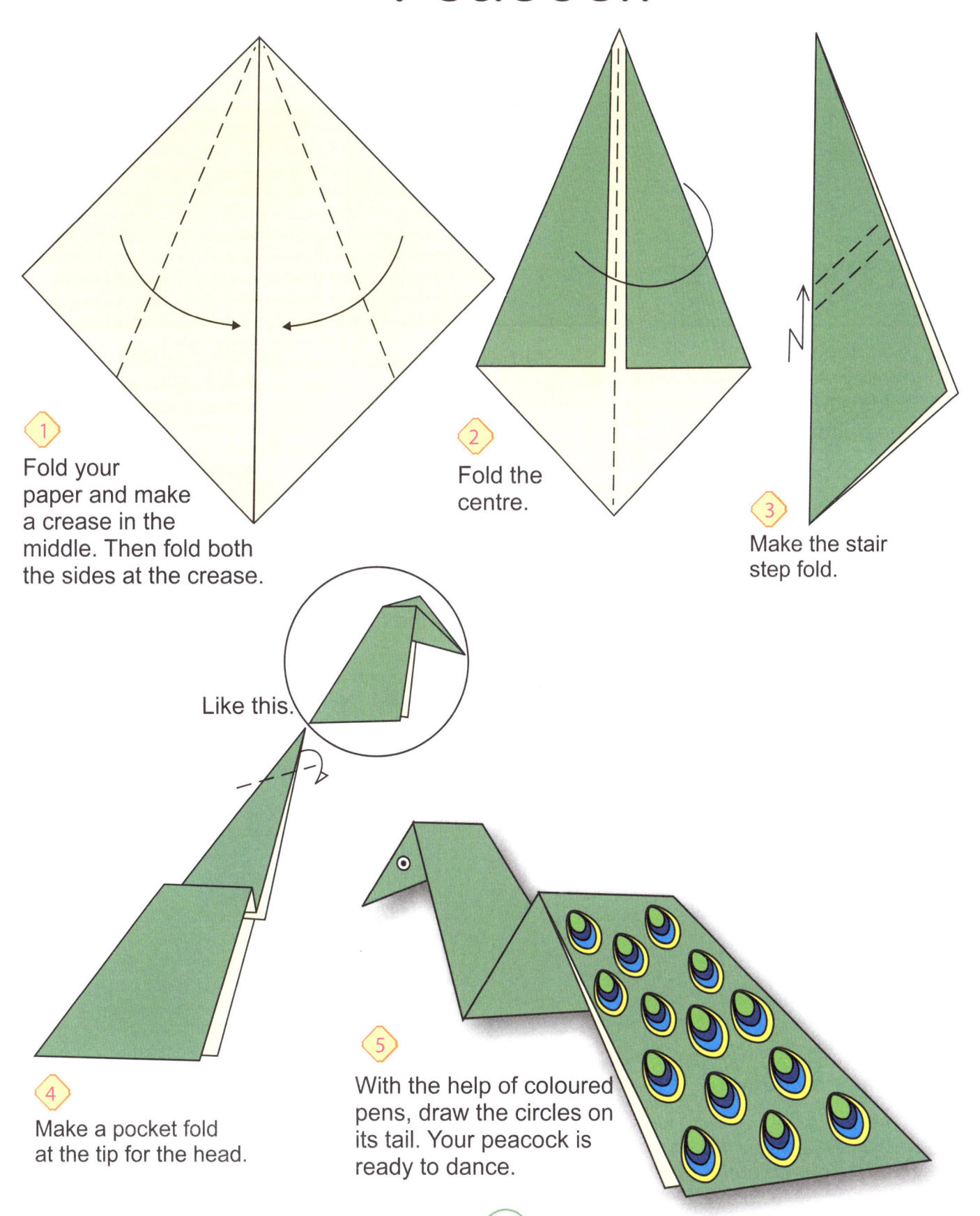

1 Fold your paper and make a crease in the middle. Then fold both the sides at the crease.

2 Fold the centre.

3 Make the stair step fold.

Like this.

4 Make a pocket fold at the tip for the head.

5 With the help of coloured pens, draw the circles on its tail. Your peacock is ready to dance.

Fan

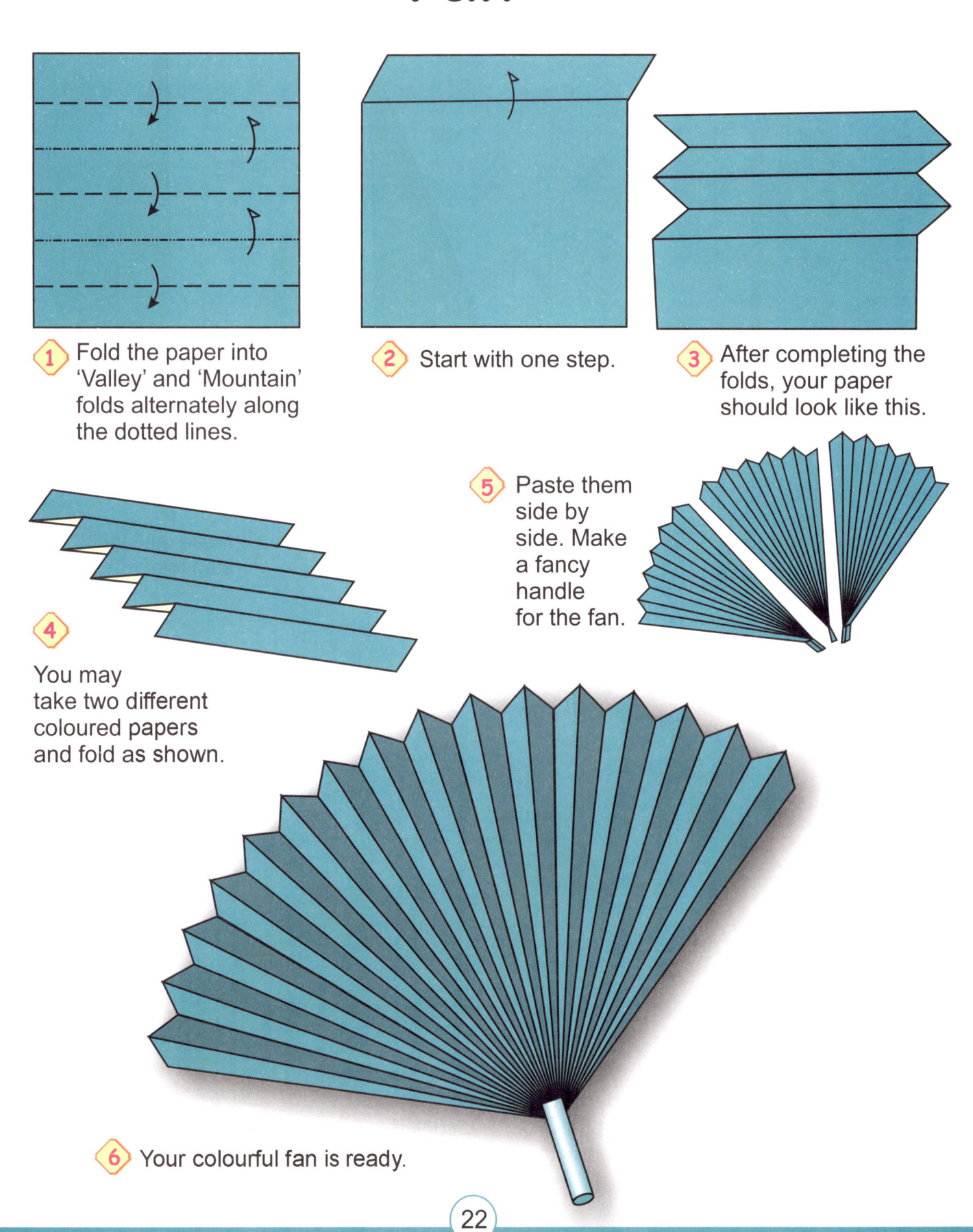

1. Fold the paper into 'Valley' and 'Mountain' folds alternately along the dotted lines.

2. Start with one step.

3. After completing the folds, your paper should look like this.

4. You may take two different coloured papers and fold as shown.

5. Paste them side by side. Make a fancy handle for the fan.

6. Your colourful fan is ready.

Piano

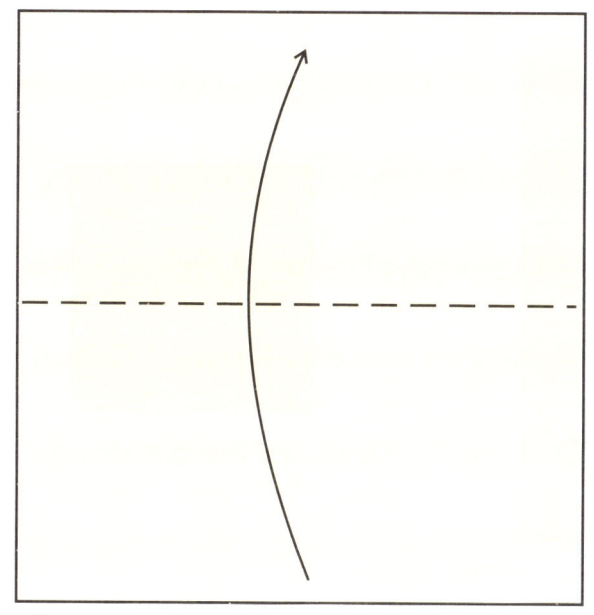

1. Fold the paper into half.

2. It will look as shown.

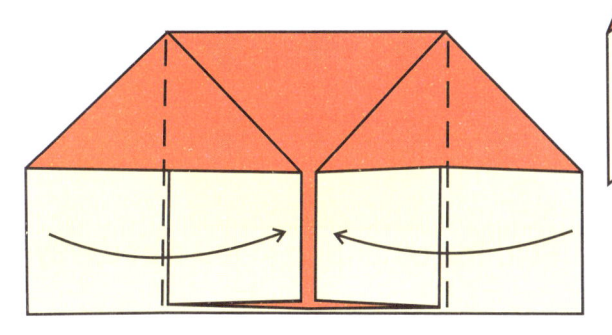

3. Fold the side flaps forward at the dotted lines to bring them at right angles at the middle square.

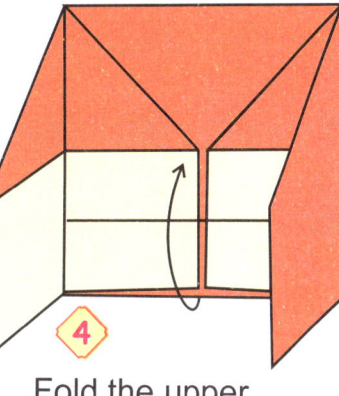

4. Fold the upper layer of the middle square.

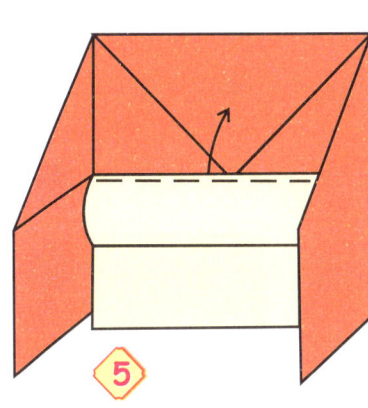

5. Fold once more and keep it in a horizontal position. It will form the keyboard of the piano.

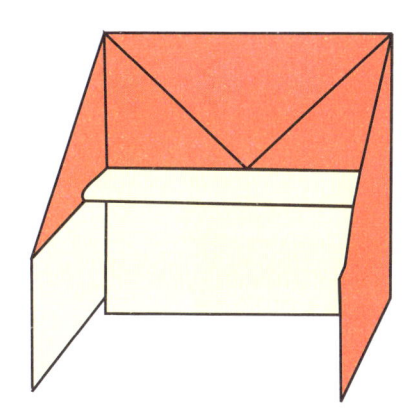

6. Draw some lines on it with a black pen.

7. Your piano is ready to be played.

Yacht

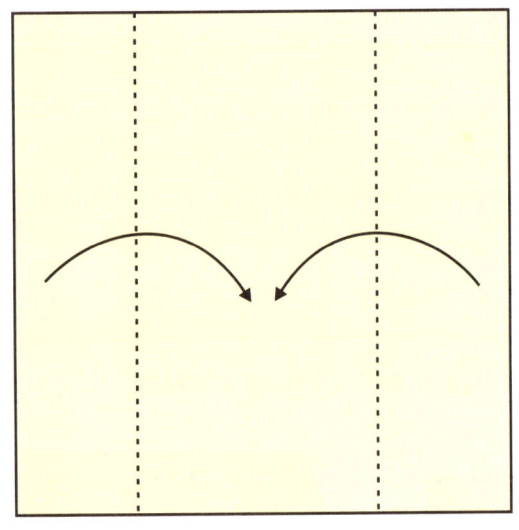

1 Fold the right and the left sides to centre.

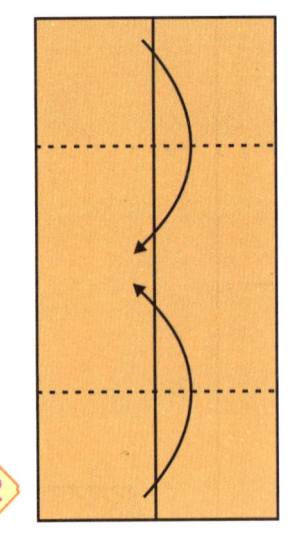

2 Fold the top and the bottom to the center is the direction of the arrow.

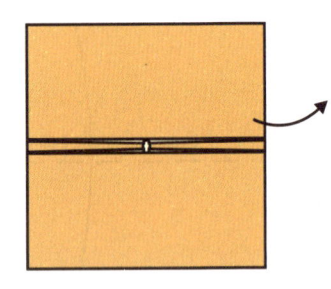

3 Open out the corner into a flattened triangle.

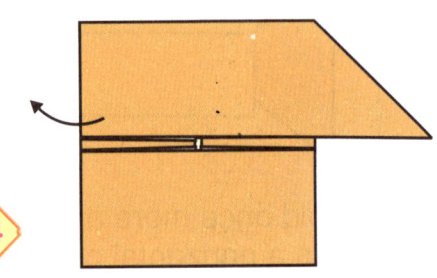

4 Fold the other side in the same way.

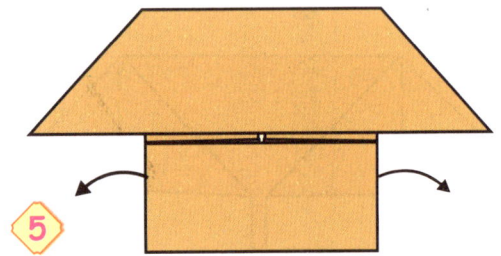

5 Fold the other part in the same way.

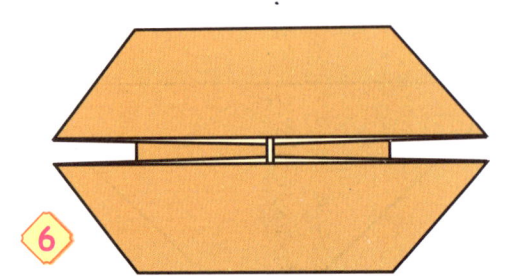

6 Your model will look like this.

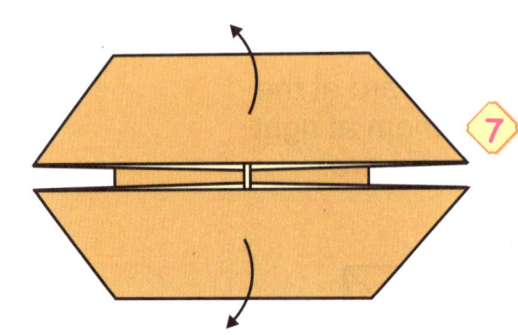

7 Open the figure on both sides in the direction of the arrows.

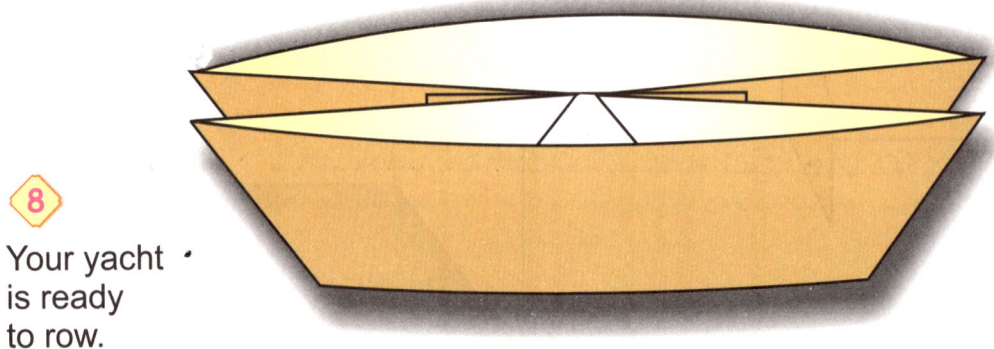

8 Your yacht is ready to row.

24